W9-BSU-811

AMERICA the BEAUTIFUL

MICHIGAN

By R. Conrad Stein

Consultants

Louis Romano, Professor, College of Education, Michigan State University, East Lansing

Thomas L. Jones, Executive Director, Historical Society of Michigan, Ann Arbor

Robert L. Hillerich, Ph.D., Bowling Green State University, Bowling Green, Ohio

CHILDRENS PRESS ®

CHICAGO

Peterson's Mill at Saugatuck

Project Editor: Joan Downing
Assistant Editor: Shari Joffe
Design Director Margrit Fiddle
Typesetting: Graphic Connections, Inc.
Engraving: Liberty Photoengraving

Library of Congress Cataloging-in-Publication Data

Stein, R. Conrad.
    America the beautiful, Michigan.

    (America the beautiful state books)
    Includes index.
    Summary: Introduces the geography, history,
government, economy, industry, culture, historic sites,
and famous people of this state composed of two
peninsulas more or less surrounded by Great Lakes
water.
    1. Michigan—Juvenile literature. [1. Michigan]
I. Title. II. Series.
F566.3.S84 1987   977.4   87-9383
ISBN 0-516-00468-9

Winter in Michigan

TABLE OF CONTENTS

Chapter 1
WELCOME TO MICHIGAN

WELCOME TO MICHIGAN

"Nothing is so certain as change," according to a French proverb. This old saying aptly describes the complex state of Michigan.

From the beginning, Michigan's people and institutions have shifted in form and focus like some of the lovely sand dunes that line its lakeshore. Michigan's economy was once dominated by fur trading. Then mining became important, followed by logging, farming, manufacturing, and eventually high-tech industry. The state's land was occupied first by Indians, then by the French, next by the British, and finally by the Americans. For a brief moment in history, even the Spanish laid claim to a small corner of Michigan.

The winds of change brought in waves of people. Pioneers came from the eastern United States and from northern Europe. Later settlers migrated from southern Europe, the southern United States, and the Latin American countries.

Michigan's landscape reflects the shifts of its history. The state was a vast forest until loggers laid its face almost bare. Farmers followed the loggers. Railroads crisscrossed the fields. Towns grew and factories sprouted up.

"Welcome to Michigan" signs are posted along the dozens of roads that cross its borders. It is an exciting state, filled with lovely scenery, friendly people, and interesting things to do and see. While reading its story, expect to be taken on a roller-coaster ride. Changes, both sudden and dramatic, dominate the saga of Michigan.

Chapter 2
THE LAND

THE LAND

The Michigan state motto, "If you seek a pleasant peninsula, look about you," extols Michigan's scenery; it also uses the key word "peninsula." A peninsula is a body of land surrounded on three sides by water. Michigan is divided into the Upper Peninsula and the Lower Peninsula, both of which are surrounded by Great Lakes waters. The two peninsulas are separated by the Straits of Mackinac, where Lake Michigan and Lake Huron converge. Only the islands of Hawaii present a more radical geographic division within a state.

LAND AREA

The Upper Peninsula (also called the U.P. or Upper Michigan) is about one-fourth the size of the Lower Peninsula. The Lower Peninsula (also called Lower Michigan) is shaped like a giant mitten that is waving north, toward Canada. The bulge of land jutting into Lake Huron at Saginaw Bay is referred to as "Michigan's thumb."

The state's land area spreads over 58,527 square miles (151,584 square kilometers). In size, it ranks twenty-third in the United States and is the third-largest state east of the Mississippi River. While not the biggest state, it is one of the most sprawling. A drive from Ironwood in the northwestern corner of the Upper Peninsula to Detroit in southeastern Lower Michigan is as long as a car trip from Detroit to New York City.

The north shore of the Upper Peninsula is washed by the waters of Lake Superior (left). Boulder-covered fields throughout the state (right) were left by the last retreating glacier.

Dozens of islands that dot the lake waters are part of Michigan's territory. Some contain rural communities that live in proud isolation from the rest of the state. The largest of the islands is the rugged and scenic Isle Royale. A splendid nature reserve and national park, it can be reached only by boat or seaplane.

TOPOGRAPHY AND GEOGRAPHY

About ten thousand years ago, the last glacier retreated from North America and left Michigan with a permanently wrinkled face. Endless hills ripple its surface, though there are few dramatic valleys or suddenly rising mountains. Only in the northwest corner of the Upper Peninsula does one find mountains.

Michigan shares common borders with Indiana, Ohio, and Wisconsin, and its shores are washed by four of the five Great Lakes. In addition to the American states, Canada is also a next-door neighbor. Canada is so entwined with Michigan that one has to drive south to get from downtown Detroit to Windsor, Ontario. This is the only spot along the United States-Canada border where one travels south to get from the United States to Canada.

THE FORESTS

Before European settlers arrived, most of Michigan was covered by a majestic cloak of trees. A squirrel could scamper across the northern Lower Peninsula on branches alone, never once touching the ground. The trees were so tall and so dense that to walk through them even at high noon meant walking in the dark.

Then, in the mid-1800s, came the loggers. In their wake they left fields of stumps. Devastating forest fires also took their toll. Today the original trees that greeted the European explorers exist only in small groves such as the one found at Hartwick Pines State Park in northern Lower Michigan.

But it is a mistake to think of Michigan's woodlands only in the past tense. Forests of second and later growth cover more than half of modern Michigan. Pines and hardwood trees sprawl over twenty million acres (eight million hectares) in the northern half of the Lower Peninsula and most of the Upper Peninsula. About twelve million acres (nearly five million hectares) are owned by private lumber companies. The remainder are part of Michigan's vast state and national forest system.

Today's commercial forests are managed, rather than stripped by the cut-and-run methods of the past. Modern Michigan foresters plant more trees each year than they cut down. One

Forests cover more than half the state.

wonders how Michigan would look if loggers of an earlier era had practiced some form of conservation.

THE LAKE SHORES

Michigan is the keystone of the Great Lakes; four of the five Great Lakes wash its shores. Though it may seem peculiar to think of midwestern Michigan as a maritime state, the Detroit River and the locks at Sault Sainte Marie are among the busiest waterways in the world.

The state's lakeshore towns have a "seafaring" society much like that found along the Massachusetts shore. Crusty old sailors in these towns claim that Great Lakes storms are more treacherous

Lighthouses (right), dot the shores of the Great Lakes. A lifeboat from the *Edmund Fitzgerald* (below), a ship that sank in 1975, is a reminder of the treacherous storms that spring up on the Great Lakes.

than those in the North Atlantic. They talk in hushed tones of some of the more recent tragedies of the lakes—the iron-ore carrier *Daniel Morrell* that went down during a gale in 1966, and the *Edmund Fitzgerald* that sank with all hands in November 1975.

Michigan's shorelines are also famous for their amazing variety and spectacular natural beauty. In the Upper Peninsula, where the northern coast stretches along Lake Superior, the scenery is wild and rugged. On the Lake Michigan shore in the Lower Peninsula rise the rolling sand dunes that delight tourists. Thick forests are featured on the state's east coast along Lake Huron.

RIVERS AND INLAND LAKES

In Michigan, one is never more than six miles (ten kilometers) from a river, stream, or lake. It is not surprising, therefore, that the state has long been known as the "Water Wonderland." If all of Michigan's rivers came together to form one continuous stream, that stream would be long enough to wrap all the way around the

Bond Falls, on the Ontanagon River in the Upper Peninsula

earth at the equator. More than fifteen thousand inland lakes dot Michigan's farm and forest lands.

Along Michigan's borders, the Detroit, Saint Clair, and Saint Mary's rivers are major avenues of shipping. The Grand River in the Lower Peninsula flows for 260 miles (418 kilometers) and is the longest in the state. Other prominent Lower Peninsula rivers are the Au Sable, Clinton, Huron, Kalamazoo, Manistee, Muskegon, Raisin, and Saginaw. Upper Peninsula rivers include the Escanaba, Manistique, Ontonagon, and Tahquamenon. The Lower Peninsula boasts the state's largest inland lake, the 30-square-mile (77.7-square-kilometer) Houghton Lake.

Strangely, with all its rivers and hills, Lower Michigan has but one waterfall—the Ocqueoc, near Rogers City. On the other hand, the Upper Peninsula has more than 150 waterfalls. The most spectacular are the upper and lower falls of the Tahquamenon River. A series of waterfalls with an even taller total drop tumbles near the city of Marquette. It has the picturesque name Laughing Whitefish Falls.

These ducks and migrating Canada geese are among the hundreds
of species of birds that spend at least part of the year in Michigan.
Isle Royale National Park is home to a large herd of moose.

WILDLIFE

Michigan's deer population approaches one million animals—
more deer than in any other state except Texas. Though
Michigan's elk were hunted into extinction long ago, in 1918
authorities planted a herd of seven elk in the forests of the
northern Lower Peninsula. The elk survived and flourished; there
are now hundreds of elk in the state. A herd of six hundred to
eight hundred moose lives in Isle Royale National Park. Also
living at Isle Royale is one of the nation's last packs of timber
wolves.

Though Michigan is called the Wolverine State, no wolverines
live there. It is likely that the animal never has lived within the

16

boundaries of the state. Long ago, French trappers may have brought wolverine pelts into the area to trade with Indians, and hence the name. Beavers, prized for their pelts, played an important role in the economy of early Michigan, however, and some people believe the state should be named after that industrious animal. Other fur-bearing animals that live in Michigan include badgers, otters, mink, foxes, skunks, muskrats, and raccoons. Lumbering black bears and sleek bobcats dwell in the forests. Countless species of birds nest in the state. The autumn skies are laced with formations of migrating geese.

FARMLAND

About 30 percent of the state's land is devoted to farming. Michigan's most productive and most numerous farms lie in the southern third of the Lower Peninsula. A long strip of land hugging the Lake Michigan shore is ideally suited for fruit growing. Farms become fewer and forests take over as one travels farther north in the Lower Peninsula. In the Upper Peninsula, an unforested area is rarely seen. Still, dairy farms and cattle-raising operations are carried on throughout the rugged Upper Peninsula.

CLIMATE

Most people think of Michigan as a land of severe winters. However, the Lower Peninsula is protected from arctic chills by the surrounding Great Lakes waters. During the summers the lake waters turn warm and are slow to cool even when winter temperatures arrive. Thus, the warmth of the lakes takes some of the bite out of winter's winds. The reverse of this effect tends to "air condition," or cool off, Michigan's summers.

Snowfall is heaviest in the Upper Peninsula.

While the lake waters moderate Michigan's climate—particularly that of the Lower Peninsula—the state still experiences weather extremes. Records were set in 1934 when the mercury plunged to minus 51 degrees Fahrenheit (minus 46 degrees Celsius) in Vanderbilt and in 1936 when it reached a sweltering 112 degrees Fahrenheit (44 degrees Celsius) at the town of Mio.

Michigan's many rivers and lakes are evidence that the state enjoys ample rainfall. Droughts occur, but only rarely. Snowfall is heaviest in the Upper Peninsula. A record year for snowfall came in the winter of 1978-79; 355.9 inches (9 meters) of snow blanketed the area of Houghton in the Upper Peninsula. New York City ordinarily does not receive that much snow in a decade of winters.

Fall colors near Northport

Autumn is Michigan's most beautiful season. In mid-September, fall begins in the north with splashes of brilliant rust, orange, and yellow that work slowly southward. The fall colors are especially breathtaking because the state's delightful array of deciduous (leafy) trees contrasts with its many evergreens.

Late fall and early winter bring the fierce storms that howl across the Great Lakes. A popular folk song once warned Great Lakes seamen of the "Gales of November."

As spring approaches, accumulated snow melts, rivers overflow, and farmland turns to muck. Years ago, when only dirt roads connected the communities of Upper Michigan, rural schools closed for a week each spring so the school buses would not get stuck in the mire. Students called this annual spring break Mud Week.

Chapter 3
THE PEOPLE

THE PEOPLE

Michiganders live in splendid isolation. Because most of the state is surrounded by water, only a small a portion of its border directly touches other states. This geographic situation has helped give Michiganders a refreshing originality in their approach to life. Their opinions, ideals, and politics are products of their own thoughts rather than those of their neighbors. Throughout its history, therefore, Michigan has led rather than followed the nation.

POPULATION AND POPULATION DISTRIBUTION

With more than nine million people, Michigan ranks eighth among the nation's states in population. Early in this century, Michigan was one of the fastest growing states in America. That is no longer the case. From 1980 to 1990, Michigan's population increased by only 0.4 percent, compared to a national rise of 9.8 percent during the same period. In 1986, the United States Census Bureau reported that Michigan was one of five states that actually lost population in the first half of the 1980s. People left Michigan to look for opportunities in the West and the South.

Michigan is an urban state; more than three-quarters of its people live in or near cities. Only 320,000 residents (less than 4 percent of the population) live in the Upper Peninsula, yet that area has 25 percent of Michigan's land. By comparison, Detroit and its suburbs hold nearly 50 percent of the state's people in an area only about as large as an average Upper Peninsula county.

**Residents of Detroit and other southern Michigan cities enjoy
vacationing in the peace and quiet of the sparsely populated north.**

The best way to picture Michigan's population distribution is to divide the state into three parts: the Upper Peninsula and the northern Lower Peninsula; the southern Lower Peninsula minus the Detroit area; and Detroit and its suburbs.

In the Upper Peninsula and northern Lower Michigan, there are more deer and bears than there are people. Marquette, the largest city in the Upper Peninsula, has only about twenty-two thousand people and is small by most standards. Still, northern Lower Michigan and the Upper Peninsula enjoyed a small population explosion in the mid-1970s. For years, Detroiters and residents of other southern cities have owned hunting and fishing cabins in the north. During the 1970s, many urban dwellers and retirees escaped the pressures of city life and decided to live year-round at their "summer cottages." Some northern counties enjoyed a 40 percent growth rate in the decade of the 1970s.

About 90 percent of Michigan's people live in the southern half of the Lower Peninsula — in cities such as Grand Rapids (above) or in small towns such as Zeeland (left).

About 90 percent of Michigan's people live in the southern half of the Lower Peninsula. The cities of that region include Lansing, the capital; Grand Rapids, Michigan's second-largest city; and industrial centers such as Flint, Battle Creek, Saginaw, and Kalamazoo. Here, too, are dozens of quiet towns that center on a church, a courthouse, and a post office. Many were settled more than a century ago and have grown graceful with age.

In the southeastern corner of the state lies the greater Detroit area. The city of Detroit is the sixth-largest city in the United States. Its suburbs sprawl into the surrounding countryside.

Holland, a town settled by Dutch people in 1846, has an annual tulip festival.

A COSMOPOLITAN PEOPLE

On the coast of Lake Michigan lies the small city of Holland. There vendors sell wooden shoes hand carved by Old World craftspeople. On a nearby island stands a windmill that was carefully transplanted from the Netherlands. Its whirling blades are as high as a twelve-story building. During the annual tulip festival, Holland's population of nearly thirty-one thousand swells to half a million. Holland is the spiritual capital of Michigan's Dutch people, most of whose ancestors migrated to Michigan in the last century. Other European ethnic areas include Finns in the Upper Peninsula, Germans in several southern towns, Greeks in Detroit, and Poles in Detroit's suburbs.

Nearly 14 percent of Michigan's population is made up of black people, most of whom live in the Detroit area. More than 75

About 1.2 million people
live in Detroit,
Michigan's largest city.

percent of Detroit's population is black. Sizable black communities
are also found in other southern industrial centers. In contrast,
there are few black residents in the mostly rural Upper Peninsula
and northern Lower Peninsula.

Almost 400,000 foreign-born people live in Michigan. The
largest group comes from Canada. Most other foreign-born
residents are Europeans such as Britons, Poles, Germans, and
Dutch.

Though Michigan was once entirely the domain of Indians,
Native Americans now make up less than 1 percent of the state's
population; they live in both urban and rural areas.

Michigan's diverse groups practice a host of religions. Roman
Catholics form the largest religious body. They are followed by

Baptists, Episcopalians, Lutherans, and Methodists. Jewish synagogues can be found in nearly all of Michigan's cities. Mormons, Seventh Day Adventists, Dutch Reformed, Amish, and Muslims also played a role in the state's history. A relatively new Christian sect, the House of David, was founded in Benton Harbor early in the twentieth century.

REGIONALISM

Many residents of the Upper Peninsula feel that their piece of land, so geographically distinct from the Lower Peninsula, should be politically distinct from it as well. They have considered forming a separate state, which could be called Superior, or joining Wisconsin, because they believe the Upper Peninsula has more in common with that state than with much of the Lower Peninsula. This sentiment is strongest in the western half of the Upper Peninsula. Though the voices advocating such changes have never been in the majority, the suggestion indicates the pressure of regionalism in Michigan.

The southern Lower Peninsula, aside from Detroit, was settled by New Yorkers and New Englanders who began migrating to Michigan in the 1830s. They brought with them a love of political order and a respect for education.

Detroit and its ring of suburbs is home to "city people," men and women with aspirations different from those who grew up on farms.

The people of the rural north, as might be expected, resent paying taxes to fund services that benefit the Detroit area. This resentment is heightened by the fact that historically Detroit is the seat of wealth and power. For their part, the city dwellers point out that Detroit residents pay the bulk of the state's taxes. The rifts are eased through communication; most citizens travel extensively within the state, and this allows farmers and city people to exchange ideas.

POLITICAL MICHIGAN

Describing Michigan's political climate is like trying to describe a typical Michigan citizen. A mold does not exist. The mood of the state's voters shifts easily from conservative to liberal to middle-of-the-road. These variable voting patterns not only keep politicians alert, but also frustrate the so-called experts who claim they can predict political trends.

Michigan voters seem to delight in defying the mood of the country. During the Democrats' golden years—the 1960s and early 1970s—Michigan elected Republican governors. When the Republican party captured the nation in the 1980s, Michigan chose a Democrat to be its governor. During election years, "big business" donates money to pro-business Republican candidates. At the same time, large labor unions urge their members to vote for Democrats who are friendly to labor. But no one can tell a Michigander how to vote. Despite the efforts of the powerful labor unions, Michigan had voted for Republican presidential candidates since the 1960s—until 1992, when it backed Democrat Bill Clinton. And, to the chagrin of big business, the state had two liberal Democratic senators in the 1980s.

The only somewhat predictable element of political Michigan is the influence of regionalism on the voters. Generally, the rural north votes for Republicans, while city dwellers and the Upper Peninsula prefer Democrats. But in Michigan the exception is the norm, and it surprises no one when farm people rally behind a Democrat or city folk champion a Republican.

Chapter 4

EARLY MICHIGAN

EARLY MICHIGAN

"Wassamo was living with his parents on the shores of a large bay on the east coast of Lake Michigan. It was at a period when nature spontaneously furnished everything that was wanted, when the Indians used skins for clothing, and flints for arrowheads. It was long before the time that the flag of the white man was seen in these lakes, or the sound of an iron axe had been heard."

Thus begins a story told by Ottawa Indians about Michigan's ancient era. The tale was put into writing by Henry Rowe Schoolcraft, a famous Michigan resident who lived in the Upper Peninsula in the early 1800s. The legend tells of the heroic time when Indian people were masters of all Michigan.

THE FIRST MICHIGANDERS

Archaeologists believe that human beings have lived on Michigan's two peninsulas for at least twelve thousand years. Michigan's prehistoric residents were descendants of the primitive hunters who crossed the Bering Strait from Asia to what is now Alaska. At the time, glacial ice still covered most of North America. Those hardy men and women who crossed the forbidding icescape were the true discoverers of the New World.

As the ice retreated, the climate gradually warmed and forests sprouted up in Michigan. The ancient people hunted deer, moose, and caribou while slowly learning the art of farming. Corn and squash became staple crops. Tools such as stone axes to clear trees and bowls to grind corn appeared in the villages.

Around 3,000 B.C., the people of northern Michigan learned to fashion copper into knives and harpoon tips. They found the copper ore in the hills of the Keweenaw Peninsula and at Isle Royale in Lake Superior. Today, hikers at Isle Royale can see ruins of a prehistoric copper mine. Some historians suggest that Michiganders were the earliest metalworkers in the world.

Several centuries before the Christian era, a culture archaeologists call the Mound Builders developed in Illinois and Ohio and spread to southern Michigan. These people built large mounds of loose earth for burial or worship. The largest surviving group of authentic mounds found in Michigan rise from the ground along the Grand River just west of Grand Rapids. Those mounds date back about two thousand years.

For unknown reasons, the mound-building cultures died out in the midwestern United States in the 1500s. This is also the era that historians call the "contact period"—the time when the Native Americans, who came to be called Indians, first met Europeans. That meeting changed the life-style of the Indians more dramatically than anyone could have dreamed.

THE THREE FIRES

At the time when Europeans touched upon America's east coast, about a hundred thousand people lived in the Great Lakes region. The prominent culture groups in Michigan included the Chippewa and Menominee in the Upper Peninsula, and the Miami, Ottawa, and Potawatomi in Lower Michigan. A group called the Wyandot lived in the Detroit area.

Isle Royale may have been the first place in North America where copper was mined. This prehistoric copper pit was probably mined around 3000 B.C.

The Potawatomi, the Chippewa, and the Ottawa, Michigan's dominant groups, formed a loose confederation called the Three Fires. While their economies and day-to-day living habits were different, all three groups spoke Algonquian dialects, shared a common cultural tradition, and recognized their common cultural roots.

The Ottawa, who lived in the Upper Peninsula and the northern tip of the Lower Peninsula, were talented traders. Their tribal name, "*Adawe*," means "to trade or barter." Though all Great Lakes Indians were skilled canoeists, the Ottawa reigned supreme. Their trading parties ranged through inland rivers and along the perilous shores of the Great Lakes.

Chippewa Indians were still fishing Michigan waters from birchbark canoes (above) when these pictures were taken in 1938. Right: A Chippewa woman sets fishing nets out to dry.

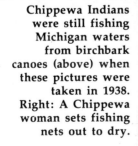

The Chippewa, of the northern Lower Peninsula, were the largest group in the Three Fires confederation. The short growing season limited their crop production, so the Chippewa lived largely on game or fish. They used cleverly crafted nets to catch and haul in sturgeon, whitefish, and perch. In autumn they hunted deer and moose in their forest-covered land.

The Potawatomi were the most advanced farmers of the Three Fires. Their traditional territory lay to the south, still Michigan's richest farming area. The land there was not as heavily forested as that in the north, and the Potawatomi burned away grass and brush to clear fields for planting. Their principal crops were corn, beans, squash, and tobacco. After harvest time, the Potawatomi moved their villages into the thick forests of the north to find protection from the biting winds of winter.

The Indians who lived in the Michigan region held a number of religious beliefs in common. They believed that a supreme being created the universe and that minor spirits controlled the lesser elements, such as winds and lake tides. They might offer presents to gain the friendship of the spirits of the forest or the water.

The Indians endured Michigan's often hostile environment by sharing their food and shelter. Before the arrival of the explorers and pioneers, selfishness and greed among themselves were rare. In their villages no one went homeless, and if one person's stomach rumbled from hunger, that meant everyone was hungry—even the village leaders.

We do not know just when Michigan's Indians first learned that bands of curious strangers were traveling the continent. Considering the Indians' skill as canoeists and traders, however, it is logical to assume that some hint of white people's presence reached Michigan years before the first European approached its shores.

Chapter 5
UNDER THE BANNER OF CONQUERORS

UNDER THE BANNER OF CONQUERORS

In a southern Michigan town called Niles is a hotel with the unusual name Four Flags. Nearby is the Four Flags Beauty Shop, the Four Flags Used Car Lot, and the office of the Four Flags Area Chamber of Commerce. Niles stands at the site of an old fort built by Europeans. During the fort's history, the flags of four different nations—France, Great Britain, Spain, and the United States—have flown above its pine ramparts. The four flags of Niles are reminders that change is the theme of the Michigan story.

THE FRENCH COME TO MICHIGAN

Far to the east of Michigan, the French constructed a series of fortress towns along the banks of the Saint Lawrence River in present-day Canada. The French believed that somewhere in North America was an undiscovered waterway that would allow a sailing vessel to pass through the continent, emerge into the Pacific Ocean, and sail on to China. Exploring parties sailed west from French settlements to search for this elusive "Northwest Passage."

Around 1618, a young adventurer named Étienne Brulé and one companion undertook an incredible canoe journey. Paddling his frail craft along the Great Lakes, Brulé penetrated the wilds of North America and became the first European to gaze at the shores of Michigan.

Next, another Frenchman, Jean Nicolet, sailed through the

Straits of Mackinac and entered the lake the Chippewa called Michigama, meaning "great lake." Nicolet was so confident he would reach China that he packed a colorful silk robe to wear when he touched upon that country's shores. Instead, Nicolet landed at what is now Green Bay, Wisconsin, where a number of Indians were enthralled by the fine silk garment.

The search for the Northwest Passage continued for a century. No such easy waterway existed in North America, but the quest for it blazed new trails in the wilderness.

Soon after the early explorers came missionaries who carried the Christian message to the Indians. Many of the missionaries were familiar with mapmaking, and their notes and sketches helped to chart the Great Lakes. The earliest missionary in Michigan was Father René Ménard, who established a mission at Keweenaw Bay in the Upper Peninsula in 1660. Eight years later, the Jesuit priest Jacques Marquette built a church at the rapids that the French called Sault Sainte Marie. It was a perfect spot for a church because paths along the riverbank were trade routes for hundreds of Indians and Europeans. Father Marquette's mission church was the first permanent European settlement in Michigan.

In the late 1600s, adventurer René-Robert Cavelier, Sieur de La Salle, left his mark on Michigan. He built a string of forts along the shores of the Great Lakes, including a log stockade called Fort Miami that stood near the present-day city of Saint Joseph. Hoping to grow wealthy in the fur trade, La Salle constructed a ship called the *Griffon* that was designed to haul fur pelts. The *Griffon* was the first vessel other than a canoe to sail the Great Lakes. In November 1679, La Salle waited at Fort Miami for the *Griffon* to return from its maiden voyage. His wait was in vain, for the ship was never seen again. It was the first large vessel to fall victim to Lake Michigan's "gales of November."

French adventurer La Salle (left), who explored the Great Lakes region in 1669, built a string of forts along the shores of the lakes, including one near the present-day city of Saint Joseph.

Today we associate the name Cadillac with a luxury automobile, but history hails Antoine de la Mothe Cadillac as the founder of the city of Detroit. A soldier and fortune-seeker, Cadillac commanded a group of Frenchmen who built Fort Pontchartrain on the north bank of the Detroit River in 1701. No one in the group could have known that their wilderness settlement would grow into one of the world's most important industrial centers.

THE FUR TRADE

The beaver is an industrious, intelligent animal. The dams beavers build for shelter help prevent rivers from overflowing and provide quiet waters suitable for schools of young fish. Instead of respecting the beaver, however, people have made it the most hunted animal of the modern era. The beaver's fur is soft and shiny and wears well. The highly prized fur was in such demand for coats and hats that the European beaver was hunted to near-

Fort Michilimackinac in Mackinaw City was built by the French during the early years of the North American fur trade when Michigan was in French hands.

extinction by the 1500s. Then the French discovered that the New World, especially the Great Lakes region, was rich with beavers. The brisk winters meant that other fur-bearing animals such as mink, fox, and muskrat also could provide fine pelts. For more than two centuries, fur dealers carried on a lucrative and aggressive trade between the New World and the Old—all at the expense of these animals.

In the early years of the North American fur trade, France expanded its fort complexes at the Great Lakes straits through which all boats had to pass. Important French forts stood at Detroit and the Straits of Mackinac. The French flew their flags over these strategically placed stockades and Michigan was securely in French hands.

The fur trade had a powerful impact on the lives of the Indians. To obtain the newcomers' goods, Indians worked for the French as trappers. Records indicate that a flintlock gun usually cost an Indian trapper twelve beaver pelts. The ultimate cost to the Indian was much greater, for trading with the French led to the destruction of the traditional Indian way of life. The Potawatomi, Michigan's most advanced farmers, abandoned their fields for the woods. Trapping replaced farming, and soon the Indians relied heavily on the Europeans for even the necessities of life.

The fur trade was so lucrative that it finally upset the lives of the French. Peasants who traveled to Michigan to start farms quickly learned of the profits to be had from furs. Many went into the forests to trap animals themselves or to trade with those who did. Finally, the fur trade shook the capitals of old Europe. Competition between British and French fur dealers was one of the causes of the Seven Years' War that broke out in 1756. Although that war raged between France and England, it spilled over into the New World, where it is known as the French and Indian War. The war ended in 1763, a resounding defeat for the French.

The British victory meant the fall of the North American empire called New France. It had begun during the 1600s and had lasted about 150 years. During that time, the Michigan region changed very little. Under French rule, only a few established farms operated, most of them along the Detroit River. However, New France was characterized by peaceful mingling between Indians and whites. Many French trappers and traders married Indian women and raised families. The next rulers of Michigan treated the land and the people in a profoundly different manner.

THE BRITISH PERIOD

Against the rat-a-tat-tat of drums and the whistle of fifes, red-coated British troops proudly raised the Union Jack flag above the ramparts of Michigan's forts. The new flags fluttering high over the stockades meant that British power had come to the Great Lakes region.

The Indians felt the change immediately. For decades, for example, the French had followed the traditional Indian custom of showing friendship by giving gifts to Indian leaders. The British, however, saw this custom as weakness on the part of authority and would have nothing to do with it. "[The gifts] I can by no means agree to," wrote British Governor General Lord Amherst, "nor can I think it necessary to give them any presents by the way of Bribes, for if they do not behave properly they are to be punished."

The brilliant Ottawa leader Pontiac attempted to unite the various Indian groups and fight the British. Pontiac was friendly with the French, disliked and distrusted the British, but most of all wanted the Indians to remain custodians of the Great Lakes region.

A gifted military commander, Pontiac knew that his men would be slaughtered if they attempted to storm the forts. So he used clever planning to get inside the barricades. At Detroit, Pontiac and about forty warriors approached the stockade doors asking to meet with the military commander. Hidden beneath the men's blankets were tomahawks and sawed-off muskets. British Major Gladwin, however, was warned of the trick, and kept his soldiers at full military alert. A frustrated Pontiac had his men surround the fort. He hoped that French fur trappers would assist him in an attack.

The help never arrived, however, and Pontiac was forced to abandon his siege of Detroit, which had lasted from May to November of 1763. Pontiac's uprising was the last major offensive the Indians of Michigan were able to mount.

MICHIGAN BECOMES AMERICAN

Far to the east, in the colony of Massachusetts, gunfire crackled in the towns of Lexington and Concord. The great American Revolution had begun. Though no important battles were fought

Ottawa leader Pontiac (right) was unable to take the fort at Detroit by trickery (left) because the British had been told about the plan.

on Michigan soil, the British used their base at Detroit to supply the few Indian groups they had coaxed to fight on the king's side.

Spain was also at war with Great Britain, and in 1781 a Spanish-led force marched out of Saint Louis, Missouri, and captured the fort at what is now Niles, Michigan. Though the raid was insignificant, for twenty-four hours the banner of Spain fluttered above the stockade's walls. Forever after, the people of Niles have been able to boast that theirs was the only soil in the state of Michigan that has been claimed by four different nations.

The revolutionary war ended in 1783, but the new American republic was too weak to push the British completely out of Michigan. It was not until 1796 that the British finally surrendered the forts at Detroit and at the Mackinac Straits. During the War of 1812, the British retook the two forts and held them for about a year. Then, finally, the flag of the United States flew anew over the ramparts and never again has been replaced by another nation's banner.

Chapter 6
THE PIONEER ERA

THE PIONEER ERA

It ain't the funniest thing a man can do—
Existing in a country when it's new;
Nature—who moved in first—a good long while—
Has things already somewhat her own style.

These are the opening lines of a poem written by Will Carleton, a pioneer who lived in nineteenth-century Michigan. Carleton was such a popular poet that for years his birthday was a holiday for the state's schoolchildren.

THE TIMES OF LEWIS CASS

At the end of the War of 1812, the territory of Michigan was still the home of Indians and foreign fur traders—people who had no loyalty to the faraway capital of Washington, D.C. In fact, the region had not yet been surveyed and charted by an officer of the United States. All this changed when American President James Madison sent Lewis Cass to Michigan.

Born in New Hampshire, Cass became territorial governor of Michigan in 1813. With tireless energy, he set out with a party of thirty-eight others to explore and map a large area that included not only Michigan but also much of present-day Wisconsin. The trip covered more than 4,000 miles (more than 6,400 kilometers). Henry R. Schoolcraft served as the geologist for the Cass expedition. Schoolcraft later moved to Sault Sainte Marie, married

During the administration of Governor Lewis Cass (left), American fur merchant John Jacob Astor (above) controlled the pelt trade in the entire upper Great Lakes region.

a part-Chippewa woman, and wrote fascinating accounts of Indian life in the North Woods.

Fur trading continued to flourish during the Cass administration, but the federal government decreed that all fur merchants must be Americans. This gave an advantage to ruthless New York businessman John Jacob Astor. His American Fur Company, headquartered on Mackinac Island, controlled the pelt trade in the entire upper Great Lakes region.

When the fur-bearing animals had been hunted to the point of extinction, the Indians lost their source of income. Much of the forest game was gone, too. All the Indians had left was land. And this they were persuaded to turn over to the new white settlers for only a few thousand dollars.

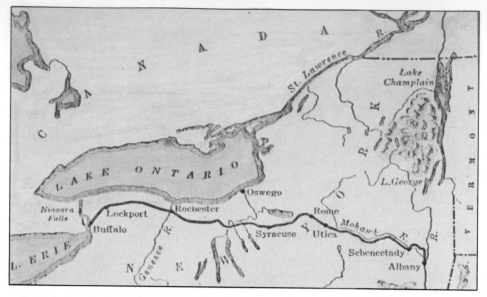

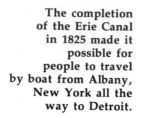

The completion of the Erie Canal in 1825 made it possible for people to travel by boat from Albany, New York all the way to Detroit.

Many of the treaties outlining the conditions of transfer of lands in the Great Lakes region had been designed by Lewis Cass. Once Michigan had been taken from the Indians, Governor Cass expected a wave of American farmers to sweep the countryside. Michigan's southern neighbors—Illinois, Ohio, and Indiana— were home to enough settlers to achieve statehood before 1820. But geography prevented pioneers from coming to Michigan. People living in the South were the most mobile Americans in the early nineteenth century. Because they discovered excellent farmland in the southern Midwest, there was no need to trek farther north. Meanwhile, farmers in the East were eager to work new lands, but were hemmed in by the Appalachian Mountains, which stood like a jagged wall from Canada to Alabama.

In addition, Michigan was haunted by government reports condemning the land as worthless. "From my observations, the Territory appears to be . . . merely a den for Indians and traders," wrote a general named Duncan McArthur, in 1814. At about the same time, land surveyor Edward Tiffin claimed that there was "not one acre in a hundred . . . that would in any case admit of cultivation." It seems astonishing today that those early observers came to such false conclusions about the rich land of Michigan.

At Lockport, Erie Canal engineers blasted five sets of double locks out of a cliff of solid rock.

THE DAWN OF SETTLEMENT

Michigan's growth began when New York State opened the Erie Canal in 1825. A 363-mile (584-kilometer) waterway, the canal cut through New York's forests, and its locks lifted barges over the mighty Appalachians. Using the canal, a family could travel by boat from Albany, New York, all the way to Detroit. A long, arduous trip was reduced to a relatively easy voyage lasting only a few weeks. Largely because of the new waterway, Michigan's population tripled during the 1820s.

Once they reached Detroit, most pioneer families moved west seeking land near what was called the Old Sauk Trail, or the Chicago Trail. The trail was rocky, stump-ridden, and scarred with deep gullies. Many wrecked wagons lined the trail, so many

47

that a Detroit newspaper claimed that the road looked like the "route of a defeated army."

Michigan's southern Lower Peninsula was settled first because there were areas of prairie land that were easier to farm than the forests of the north. New settlers had to pay the government for the land they wanted to farm as their own, but the price was low and credit was available. On reaching the new land, the pioneer family either pitched a tent or built a lean-to. Work on a permanent wood house had to wait until the first crops were harvested. Corn was a favorite crop among new immigrants. It required no plowing and could be ground into meal, a perfect food for winter months.

The New York and New England settlers were devoted letter writers and boasted of the virtues of Michigan to friends and relatives back home. Their glowing letters removed the doubts caused by negative reports that had been written by government surveyors earlier in the century. A farmer on the Huron River wrote to a friend, "The interior of Michigan is delightful—a mixture of prairies, oak openings, and woodlands, abounding in clear streams, fine lakes, and cold springs."

The settlers from the East made Michigan's pioneer period noticeably different from that of its neighbor states to the south. The easterners were village-oriented, and brought with them long-followed rules for township government. The eastern "Yankees" also had such a deep respect for education that schoolhouses sometimes were built before town halls.

STATEHOOD

Since 1787, Michigan, Ohio, Indiana, Illinois, Wisconsin, and parts of Minnesota had been lumped together in what was called the Northwest Territory. This huge land area was governed by an act of Congress called the Northwest Ordinance. The act provided that a region within the territory could apply for statehood when it reached a total population of sixty thousand. Most important, the Northwest Ordinance held that all new states would be admitted on an equal footing with the older, established, states.

Because of the waves of settlers, an 1832 census determined that eighty-six thousand people lived in the Michigan Territory, but a serious stumbling block stood in the way of statehood. Both the state of Ohio and the territory of Michigan laid claim to a strip of land that measured 75 miles (121 kilometers) long and varied between 5 and 8 miles (8 and 13 kilometers) wide. The belt of land, which included the town of Toledo, was known as the Toledo Strip. Congress delayed Michigan's statehood application until this dispute was settled.

For a time it seemed that a miniature civil war might break out between the Michigan Territory and Ohio over the Toledo Strip. Though both sides called out their militias, the soldiers did little more than shake fists at each other from opposite ends of a cornfield.

The matter was settled peacefully by the United States Congress. Ohio, already an established state, had influence in Washington and was awarded the disputed territory. As compensation, Congress gave Michigan the land that is today the western Upper Peninsula. At first, Michiganders were outraged by the terms. They argued that the bleak, nearly unknown lands to the west of the Straits of Mackinac were meager recompense for the loss of the mouth of the Maumee River and its port, Toledo. After a cooling-off period, however, a convention of delegates accepted statehood. On January 26, 1837, President Andrew Jackson signed the law making Michigan the twenty-sixth state of the Union.

The old State House in Detroit served as Michigan's capitol from 1837 to 1847, when the capital was moved to Lansing.

THE CIVIL WAR

Michigan's first governor was Stevens T. Mason. As a twenty-year-old, he had served as territorial governor, after Lewis Cass. The state's first capital was Detroit. In 1847, the capital was moved to Lansing.

In the 1850s, the explosive issue of slavery rocked America. States such as Illinois and Indiana, settled first by Southerners, had strong proslavery sentiments. The easterners who settled Michigan, on the other hand, were bitter foes of slavery. Newcomers streaming in from northern Europe also were against slavery. A few southern Michigan towns became links on the famous Underground Railroad that aided escaped slaves. The modern-day Republican party, which was formed to oppose slavery, held some of its earliest meetings in Jackson.

Although white Michiganders were generally opposed to

slavery, they were not very liberal in their treatment of blacks within the state. Before the Civil War, only a handful of free blacks lived in Michigan, yet Detroit kept its public schools strictly segregated. In an 1850 referendum, Michigan voters granted the right to vote to Indians who renounced their tribal affiliations. However, they voted against an amendment that would give voting rights to the state's blacks.

Yet, politically, Michigan sentiment remained allied with Abraham Lincoln and the Union cause. During the Civil War, ninety thousand Michiganders served in the Union forces, and fourteen thousand of them never returned home.

THE DEVELOPMENT OF INDUSTRY

Big Bill Bonifas came from Luxembourg and journeyed to Escanaba in the Upper Peninsula in the mid-1800s. He was uneducated but intelligent, and had the strength of a bear. He took a job cutting cedar trees and hauling them to the riverbank. He was paid by the tree, and while other men pulled one log, powerful Bill Bonifas hauled two. Soon Bonifas bought a horse so he could deliver even more logs. When the horse strained under the load, Big Bill slipped into a harness alongside the animal and helped to pull. Bonifas carefully saved his money and was able to bring his brothers and sisters from Europe, set up a company, and make a fortune in the lumber business.

Big Bill Bonifas was one of many pioneer businessmen who exploited Michigan resources and made a handsome living. In addition to forests for lumber, pioneers discovered that Michigan was rich in copper, iron ore, and, of course, farmland. Natural resources and the industries they spawned brought droves of new people to Michigan.

The demands of
large-scale logging
in Michigan during
the late eighteenth
century and the early
nineteenth century
spurred the expansion
of railroads.

In addition to the easterners who continued to come to Michigan, groups of European immigrants also flocked to this generous land. They came from Ireland and named the hill country near Clinton the Irish Hills. They came from The Netherlands and founded communities such as Holland in the west. Germans set up shops in many southern towns. In the Upper Peninsula, Finnish immigrants first cut trees for logging companies, then bought the barren land, pulled stumps, and started the dairy farms that their descendants still own. Swedes took work in the iron-ore mines in Marquette and the Menominee range. Scots and Welshmen extracted copper from the soil as had Michigan Indians three thousand years earlier.

The swiftly growing industries changed the face of ancient Michigan. Large-scale logging began around 1840 and lasted until 1910. Working from south to north, the army of loggers turned lush forests into stump-ridden fields. By the time of the Civil War, after only two decades of logging, three railroad lines crossed the southern half of the Lower Peninsula. Then the tracks extended northward, a boon to the lumber business. Lumbermen no longer had to wait until spring to float their logs downriver; trains could ship logs on a year-round basis.

Industry breeds industry. The demands of logging spurred the expansion of railroads. Detroit-area steel mills produced track, bridge materials, and rolling stock for the growing railroad business. The hungry furnaces of the steel industry fed on iron ore, and this need pushed the iron mines into large-scale production. Lake shipping expanded to bring ore to the mills.

Although the state suffered occasional business slumps, the close of the nineteenth century was an industrial boom era. Still, the strongest actor in Michigan's business scene had yet to take the stage.

Chapter 7
THE AGE OF THE AUTOMOBILE

THE AGE OF THE AUTOMOBILE

"Travels rough roads smoothly. A child can operate it safely. Speeds up to 25 miles an hour without fear of breakdown. Goes 40 miles on one gallon of gasoline." These glowing words advertised a 1901 "horseless carriage" called the Runabout, built by the Olds Motor Works of Detroit. Around the turn of the century, Michigan's factories began producing cars—a trickle at first, then a flood. Finally, Michigan put the world on wheels.

THE GROWTH OF THE MOTOR INDUSTRY

In the 1890s, two young men spent their spare time fussing over pistons, cylinders, and camshafts in hopes of building a passenger car they could sell to the public. Working out of his father's machine shop in Lansing, Ransom E. Olds designed a car he called the Oldsmobile. Henry Ford, who grew up on a farm in Dearborn, hammered together an automobile that was powered by a two-cylinder engine and looked like an old-fashioned buggy. Although Ford and Olds were working independently, each produced a gasoline-powered car in the year 1896.

At the time, automobiles were considered playthings for the rich. The 1901 Oldsmobile sold for $695. Inexpensive compared to most other makes, it was still out of range for the average worker. Nevertheless, more than one thousand "merry Oldsmobiles" were sold in 1904. It was the aggressive and innovative Henry Ford, however, who finally put the average person in the driver's seat.

Ford experimented with eight different models from 1903 to 1908. Finally, he created the Model T, a car that was commonly called the "Tin Lizzie." The machine was a masterpiece of simplicity and durability and became the world's most popular car. Between 1908 and 1927, more than fifteen million Model T Fords were sold.

The Model T caught the public's fancy largely because it was affordable. On Ford's assembly lines, the basic car frames moved slowly along a conveyor belt past an army of production-line employees who worked to attach parts to the chassis. At the peak of production, a new Model T was completed every twenty-four seconds. This efficiency allowed Ford to drop the price of a car from $850 to $290.

As Ford worked to improve production methods, other Michigan auto manufacturers sprang up. In 1904, the struggling Buick Car Company was bought by Flint carriage-maker "Billy" Durant and began to thrive. A decade later, the Dodge Brothers, John and Horace, graduated from producing parts for the Ford Company to making a car of their own. In 1908, Durant combined the firms that manufactured Buicks, Cadillacs, Oldsmobiles, and several other makes to form a corporate giant called General Motors. By 1920, the Michigan automobile industry was providing work for 127,000 men and women and was producing more than $1 billion worth of car parts each year. Detroit was the capital of the auto industry, but new car factories also rose in Flint, Pontiac, and Lansing.

Why did the automobile industry center almost exclusively in Michigan? Early in the industry's history, dozens of car manufacturers operated in cities throughout the Midwest. In time,

Henry Ford's first car was the quadricycle (left and top) and his most popular car was the Model T (above). In 1913, Ford cut costs—and prices—by installing moving assembly lines for production of the Model T (below).

The food-processing industry began in Battle Creek when C.W. Post and W.K. Kellogg began to produce breakfast cereals.

however, most of them were overwhelmed by the industrial might of Michigan's plants. There are several reasons for this turn of events.

First, the industry's two most daring pioneers, Ford and Olds, were native Michiganders. Second, Detroit and other Michigan towns already had factories and experienced workers. Flint, for example, had been a major producer of horse-drawn carriages. Third, Michigan was rich in the natural resources needed to build the factories as well as the automobiles. Fourth, bulky cargoes such as iron ore could be shipped with comparative ease through the Great Lakes. Finally, Michigan's financiers and lumber entrepreneurs were willing to invest money to finance plants and equipment.

Michigan's auto production continued at a breakneck pace, helping the state to grow and prosper. It even appeared that the automobile industry had helped farming—methods for building cars were applied to building tractors and other mechanical equipment. The innovations in factory methods applied to food processing as well. The food-processing industry began in Battle Creek when W.K. Kellogg and C.W. Post began to produce breakfast cereals. Farm production increased to meet the increased demands of the World War I years, yet fewer farm workers were needed. At the same time, Michigan cities and their factories were attracting young adults seeking higher wages. The population shifted away from the rural areas, and for the first time in its history, Michigan became an urban state.

THE BOOM TURNS TO BUST

The promise of jobs drew a wide variety of people into Michigan. Thousands of eastern Europeans left their crowded, impoverished homelands and migrated to Michigan's industrial towns. The most numerous of these were from Poland; by 1930, Poles were Michigan's third-largest foreign-born group. Newcomers from Italy arrived during the first quarter of the twentieth century. Mexicans came also, and filled the farm jobs that the young people of Michigan had left behind.

World War I and changes in the immigration laws discouraged the influx of Europeans, but men and women from the southern United States began to stream into Michigan. Many of these southerners were blacks seeking jobs in the industrial North. The black population of Detroit, for instance, increased from 5,741 in 1910 to 40,838 in 1920 to 120,066 in 1930. Blacks also settled in Flint, Saginaw, and Pontiac, where factory jobs were plentiful.

Two southern-born men came to Michigan and left their stamp on that state and on the world. Walter Reuther migrated from West Virginia as a teenager. He had visions of organizing industrial workers into unions powerful enough to confront the wealthy factory owners. Joe Louis Barrow, the son of a black sharecropper, was born in Alabama. The family moved to Detroit when Joe was a child. Fighting under the name Joe Louis, Barrow became what many believe to be the greatest heavyweight boxer in history. Nicknamed "the Brown Bomber of Detroit," Louis was a shining light who inspired his people during a bleak period in their history.

In 1929, the stock market crash in New York triggered the Great Depression. Millions were out of work and few had money to buy cars. Car production fell to one-fifth of its 1920s level. By 1933, more than half of Michigan's industrial workers had lost their jobs. Mayor Frank Murphy of Detroit opened abandoned warehouses to provide shelter for the city's many homeless families. The Detroit fire department cooked huge pots of soup to feed the hungry masses.

Workers who kept their jobs faced a day-to-day ordeal at the auto plants. Conditions at the plants had long been brutal. The assembly lines rolled tirelessly, while weary workers strained to perform their monotonous but exhausting tasks. As the depression lingered, wages fell and the work pace grew even more furious.

Throughout the 1930s, strikes rocked the auto factories. Some were violent, as battles broke out between workers and club-wielding police. In Flint, where General Motors officials refused to talk to union leaders, the workers staged the nation's first large-scale "sit-down strike." Workers reported to their jobs in the morning, then sat down, refused to work, and refused to leave the factories. "If the boss won't talk, don't take a walk—sit down, sit down," chanted the strikers.

In February 1937, the labor movement won an important victory when General Motors agreed to recognize the newly

When General Motors agreed to recognize the United Auto Workers in February 1937, union leaders announced the end of the sit-down strike at the Fisher Body Plant and the striking workers (above) left the premises.

organized United Auto Workers (UAW) as their employees' bargaining agent. Two months later the Chrysler Corporation made a similar agreement with the union. The aggressive UAW organizer Walter Reuther was instrumental in securing these labor pacts.

THE ARSENAL OF DEMOCRACY

"We must be the great arsenal of democracy," President Franklin Roosevelt announced on the eve of World War II. With this speech, Roosevelt launched a massive arms-production program designed to provide weapons for the war. The industrial activity needed to arm for war finally broke the grip of the depression, which had kept the American economy stagnant for a decade.

Certainly the keys to America's arsenal of democracy were in Michigan. No other state had the factories, the workers, and the

To meet the military needs of World War II, America's auto plants stopped producing civilian cars and turned to production of trucks, jeeps, and tanks.

engineers to produce thousands of trucks, tanks, and airplanes. The production of civilian cars was halted during the war years so the automotive industry could concentrate solely on making military vehicles. Before the end of the war, America's auto plants turned out 2.6 million military trucks, 600,000 jeeps, and about 50,000 tanks.

Huge new factories were built to meet the war's needs. Chrysler Company's sprawling plant in Macomb County produced a thousand tanks each month. Michigan's most impressive new plant, at Willow Run outside Detroit, was devoted to the manufacture of the B-24 bomber. Henry Ford, now nearing eighty, believed the giant four-engine plane could be made on assembly lines just as passenger cars were. Engineers argued that the bomber was far too big to be assembled like a car. Nevertheless, Ford built a huge assembly plant. Outside spread an airfield where completed bombers took off for their combat assignments. By war's end, eighty-five hundred B-24s had been built at Willow Run, and the mammoth planes had been put together on assembly lines just as Ford had directed.

In the spirit of the war effort, labor and management enjoyed a temporary truce. Led by the United Auto Workers, most unions gave voluntary no-strike pledges to the big companies. During the war the only strikes that occurred in Michigan were sporadic ones staged by smaller unions. UAW leader Walter Reuther even made suggestions to the big companies on ways to raise production.

The factories' wartime demands spread to the mines and the fields. Copper and iron-ore production increased. Prices of corn, grain, and dairy products rose to their predepression highs. But the cost of the war in human terms cannot be measured. About six hundred thousand Michigan men and women served in the armed forces; fifteen thousand of them died far from home.

THE PLIGHT OF THE BLACKS

During World War II, the United States waged a war to save democracy, yet the treatment of blacks was far from democratic. In southern states, black men in uniform were not permitted to eat in railroad dining cars even though German prisoners of war were served there. In northern states such as Michigan, white industrial workers earned record high wages, while to blacks were left the lowest-paying, most menial jobs. Of the 185 major war plants in the Detroit area, 55 hired virtually no blacks. This was despite an order by President Roosevelt requiring equal-opportunity employment in factories accepting war contracts. In such a climate of prejudice, it is no wonder that Michigan boxer Joe Louis became a larger-than-life hero and a symbol of hope for American blacks. Louis held the heavyweight crown from 1937 to 1949. In the ring he had the courage of a lion and a right hand that struck like thunder.

But people need more than heroes.

Sunday night, June 20, 1943, was a sweltering evening in

Detroit. Weary war workers lounged on park lawns trying to catch a soothing breeze. Belle Isle Park lay between a white and a black neighborhood. For years, people of both races had enjoyed the park, even though they mixed in uneasy silence. That night, a fight broke out between a white man and a black man. It was followed by another fight and then another. Police, uniformed soldiers, and gangs of young people of both races joined the brawl. The violence quickly spilled out of the park.

For two nights, rioting, looting, and racial clashes raged. State and federal troops were called in to curb the disorder. When quiet was restored, nine whites and twenty-five blacks had been killed, hundreds had been injured, and property damage totaled many thousands of dollars. It was the bloodiest of the many racial disorders in the country during the war. Bitterness between the races lingered for years afterward, both in Detroit and throughout the United States.

POSTWAR PROSPERITY

"What is good for the country is good for General Motors, and what's good for General Motors is good for the country." So said General Motors president Charles E. Wilson when he accepted a position in President Dwight D. Eisenhower's cabinet in the 1950s. The statement is often quoted because it demonstrates the confidence with which big business faced the postwar era.

After the war, Americans went on a spending spree, buying shiny big cars with engines big enough to drive trucks. Gasoline was inexpensive in those days and few people knew about air pollution or thought about safety features. Design extras such as outlandish tailfins were all the rage. These frills added to the automakers' profits. At one point during the big-car era, it cost

During the extravagant 1950s, automakers added design extras such as outlandish tailfins.

General Motors only three hundred dollars more to produce a Cadillac than a Buick, but the company knew it could sell the Cadillac for four thousand dollars more than the Buick.

Labor unions battled the auto companies for a share of the postwar prosperity. From the first agreement in 1937, Walter Reuther led the United Auto Workers from an idea to a powerful force of 1.6 million members. Reuther demanded, and often got, contracts that gave workers profit-sharing, automatic cost-of-living raises, and a salary scale guaranteeing an annual wage even if the workers were laid off. The 1948 labor contract Reuther secured with General Motors stayed in effect for more than three decades.

Several Michigan politicians rose to national prominence after the war. Democratic Governor G. Mennen Williams was considered by his party to be a serious candidate for the United States presidency in the late 1950s. He was overshadowed, however, by the charismatic John F. Kennedy of Massachusetts. In the 1960s, Republican Governor George Romney also was thought

National guardsmen exchanged shots with snipers as firemen
tried to fight a blaze during the 1967 race riots in Detroit.

of as presidential material. But Romney's poor showing in the
early presidential primaries in 1968 cooled his bid for the
presidency. In 1974, Grand Rapids Congressman Gerald Ford
became president, although he obtained the position in a
complicated, indirect way. He took office after Vice-President
Spiro Agnew and then President Richard Nixon resigned their
posts. In 1976, Ford lost a close presidential race to Jimmy Carter.

The post-war prosperity did not always paint a rosy picture for
Michigan. The 1960s came to a close on a tragic note, as another
ugly race riot wracked Detroit and spread to some other Michigan
cities. The disorders began in July 1967 and lasted a week. Detroit
shops were looted and buildings were burned. Gun battles broke
out between police and rioters. Even fire fighters were shot at.

When peace was restored, forty-three people had been killed and property damage amounted to $45 million.

Still, the overwhelming majority of Detroit's blacks remained peaceful through the bloody days of rioting. One neighborhood on the northeast side was completely spared from damage. The people in the area, almost entirely black, had converted vacant lots to parks, spent money fixing houses, and had organized block clubs. When the riots began, the people saved their neighborhood by patrolling their streets and chasing out anyone bent on violence.

MICHIGAN TODAY

In the early 1970s, newspaper headlines spelled the doom of an old way of life: "Gas Shortages Predicted." "Gas Prices Skyrocket." Finally, a front-page picture showed a forlorn-looking gas station attendant squeezing the handle on a pump nozzle and noting that nothing came out. The headline above the picture read, "Not A Drop!"

After years of squandering gasoline in monster cars, America found itself dependent on the foreign oil industry, which was controlled by the Arab-dominated cartel called OPEC (Organization of Petroleum Exporting Countries). When OPEC raised prices or slowed delivery, American drivers suffered. Suddenly the public wanted compact, gas-efficient autos. Several Detroit-based companies made compact cars, but none of the big corporations was committed to them. The demand for smaller cars caught Detroit by surprise.

American consumers turned away from Detroit and began buying small cars from foreign makers. In 1960, only 7.5 percent of Americans bought imported cars. Twenty years later that figure

The gas crisis of the early 1970s (top) created a demand for smaller, gas-efficient cars. The Detroit auto industry faltered as Americans turned to foreign makers. Even though American companies began producing compact cars (above), Michigan was losing its place as the country's major auto producer. On the other hand, the economy has been bolstered by the blossoming tourism industry and the large deposits of natural gas and oil (right) that have become important natural resources.

had jumped to 25 percent. This meant large-scale unemployment for Michigan.

Within the United States, Michigan was also losing its footing as the country's major auto producer. After World War II, auto companies began building plants in other states. By the 1980s, only one-third of American-made cars were being produced in Michigan.

"If we can't face the facts," said Michigan Governor James J. Blanchard upon taking office in January 1983, "we are going to be a state which time passes by." The facts were grim. The faltering auto industry had driven Michigan's unemployment rate well beyond the national average. In 1983, the unemployment rate was 17 percent, the state's most dismal jobless figure since the Great Depression. Loss of business and tax money forced the state government to cut some education and welfare programs.

By 1986, however, auto companies were claiming that the "period of adjustment" was over and that American-made compact cars were as fuel-efficient as foreign models. The companies also pointed out that the gas crisis had eased, making big cars practical again. Still, foreign competition continued to plague Michigan's auto industry.

A bright note in Michigan's economy was a newfound prosperity in the Upper Peninsula and the northern Lower Peninsula. Long considered an economically depressed area, Michigan's North Woods have been rediscovered by tourists. Also, oil and natural gas—discovered decades ago in the northern Lower Peninsula—have become important natural resources for the region. Many of the areas rich in oil and mineral ores, however, are part of Michigan's natural forest treasure. It will be a difficult decision to sacrifice one for the other—and the decision will affect even people who do not live in Michigan.

Chapter 8

GOVERNMENT AND THE ECONOMY

GOVERNMENT AND THE ECONOMY

Michigan's economic base has run the gamut from fur trading, to logging and mining, to farming, and finally to manufacturing. Modern Michigan is making the painful adjustment toward high-tech industries. These changes have affected all the state's institutions, including its government.

STATE GOVERNMENT

In 1963, Michigan's voters approved the state's current constitution. It models the state government after the federal government. The constitution divides authority into three separate departments or branches: the executive (the governor's office), the legislative (the state legislature), and the judicial (the court system). In theory, each department acts as a watchdog over the others.

The governor and lieutenant governor are elected as a team for a four-year term, and may be reelected any number of times. The governor makes important appointments such as state treasurer and various state department heads. The state senate must approve these appointments. The governor can also call out the state militia to assist in an emergency or to quell a disorder. In recent years, the governor has taken on the important economic and political task of persuading industries to build their factories and offices in Michigan.

Michigan State University in East Lansing (above) is the state's largest public university, and the University of Michigan in Ann Arbor (right) is the second-largest.

The state legislature consists of a 38-member senate and a 110-member house of representatives. Members are elected from districts throughout the state. Senators serve a four-year term and representatives are elected for two years. There is no limit to the number of terms a legislator may serve. The constitution gives the state legislature the power to make new laws or to rescind old ones. The governor may veto a law, but the legislature can override that veto with sufficient votes.

The judicial branch interprets laws and tries cases. Michigan's highest court is its state supreme court. It has seven justices who are elected to eight-year terms. Lesser courts include an eighteen-judge court of appeals and a circuit court.

The state's annual budget is usually arrived at only after a political battle between the governor and the legislature. Michigan's regionalism often plays a part in the budget battle. For example, conservative senators and representatives from rural areas are reluctant to approve funds to support city services.

The condition of the state's economy is a major factor in planning its budget. More than 60 percent of Michigan's revenue comes from sales taxes and income taxes. People who are out of work have no taxable income and buy few goods. So the health of the economy in a given year determines whether some state programs will continue or will have to be cut. Unfortunately, when unemployment rises and the demand for state programs increases, the state's revenue decreases.

Michigan is divided into eighty-three counties. County boards run local school systems, hire police officers, and maintain local roads. Many rural people consider their county's business to be more important than state functions.

EDUCATION

The earliest of Michigan's constitutions states, "Schools and the means of education shall forever be encouraged." Respect for education dates back to the eastern pioneer settlers. Michigan was the first state to provide free high schools, the first to appoint a superintendent of public instruction, the first to establish an agricultural college, and the first state west of the Appalachians to fund a college devoted to teacher training.

State law holds that all Michigan children must attend school from ages six through sixteen. In the 1990s, Michigan had more than 1,600,000 students enrolled in public elementary and high schools. The state spends about $6,500 per year to educate each student. Private and parochial schools serve about two hundred thousand students through grade twelve. Of the parochial schools, the Roman Catholic system is the largest.

About half a million students attend the state's thirteen public universities and twenty-nine community colleges. The largest is Michigan State University in East Lansing, America's first land-grant college; next is the University of Michigan at Ann Arbor, which is considered to be the leader in the state university system; and third largest is Wayne State in Detroit, whose charter directs the school to make a special effort to serve its urban constituency. About one-quarter of Wayne State's student body is black, and the majority of the young men and women there work their way through college by holding part-time jobs.

MANUFACTURING

Aside from autos, goods such as construction equipment and metal-working machines are major Michigan products. For more than a century, artisans in Lansing, Grand Rapids, and Muskegon have produced fine wood furniture. Kalamazoo is the state's leading paper manufacturer. Battle Creek, home of Kellogg and Post Cereals, produces more breakfast cereal and related cereal products than any other city on earth. Gerber Foods in Fremont has the country's largest baby-food plant. The largest cement plant in the United States is found at Alpena in the northern Lower Peninsula.

But even though the state's economy is more diversified than it was in the 1950s and 1960s, the automobile companies still command a leading role. In the mid-1980s, one of every three Michigan industrial workers was employed by the motor industry.

NATURAL RESOURCES

Early in the state's history, chunks of pure copper were found near the surface of the ground. Commercial copper mining began in the Upper Peninsula during the mid-1800s, and for many years Michigan led the country in production of this metal. Copper

Commercial copper mining during the mid-1800s was responsible for the growth and prosperity of Upper Peninsula towns such as Hancock, where an old copper smelter still stands on the banks of Portage Lake (left).

mining is much less important today because most of Michigan's copper ore now lies deep below the ground, and the cost of mining it exceeds the metal's market value.

The mid-1800s saw the beginning of large-scale iron mining as well. Upper Peninsula cities such as Ironwood, Iron Mountain, and Iron River grew up around the mines. Though 20 percent of the nation's iron ore still comes from mines in the Upper Peninsula, other states now produce more tons of ore than Michigan.

In the snowy forests of the northern Lower Peninsula, it is surprising to hear men and women talking in Texas drawls. But oil drilling is a growing industry in the north, and Texans are lending their expertise. Michigan has almost four thousand oil-producing wells. Natural gas, which is vital for heating homes, schools, and factories, is often found in or near oil deposits.

Perhaps the state's most outstanding natural resource is its fresh water. The Great Lakes form the world's largest reservoir of fresh water. This vast source of water—plus the state's countless rivers, inland lakes, and streams—leads many experts to claim that

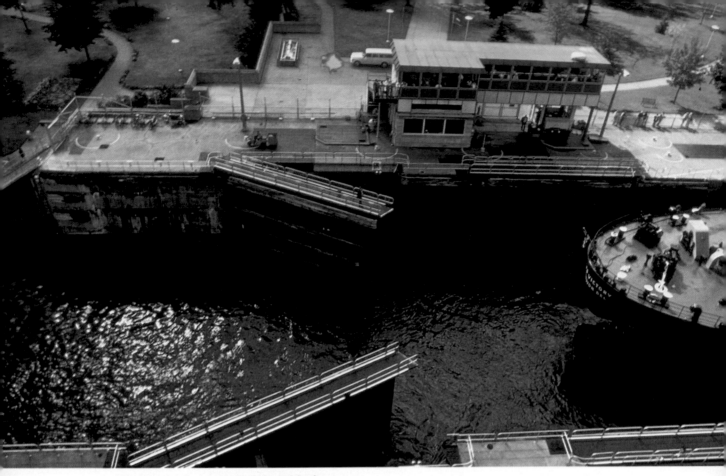

The Soo Locks at Sault Sainte Marie

Michigan is the most fortunate place on earth because it will always have access to water.

TRANSPORTATION AND COMMUNICATION

The canal at Sault Sainte Marie is the most important avenue for the hundreds of iron-ore carriers that move through the Great Lakes. Commonly called the Soo Locks, it connects Lake Superior with Lake Huron. Because Lake Superior is twenty feet (six meters) higher than its neighboring lake, the locks ease ships from one body of water to the other. During World War II, the military considered the Soo Locks to be so vital a waterway that twenty thousand troops were stationed there to protect it from possible acts of sabotage. For eight months a year, the Soo is tremendously busy. Even though winter ice halts shipping from December to mid-April, the canal is one of the world's busiest waterways.

A century ago, railroads were the most exciting of Michigan's industries. Thousands of children dreamed of someday working on the chugging giants and seeing the country from silver rails. Though railroads still haul bulky raw materials such as coal and iron ore, the industry has lost its glamor. Trucks now speed over the highways, and most passengers drive, take buses, or even fly between Michigan cities. Today passenger trains serve only ten Michigan cities.

In 1909, Michigan built the nation's first concrete highway near downtown Detroit. The roadway was only 1 mile (1.6 kilometers) long, but motorists hailed it as a miracle. In the mid-1980s, the state highway department maintained 120,000 miles (193,121 kilometers) of roads. Now only snarled traffic jams slow motorists down.

The state's most famous bridge is the mighty Mackinac, which was completed in 1957 and links the Upper and Lower Peninsula. Other noteworthy bridges include the graceful International Bridge, which spans the Saint Mary's River at Sault Sainte Marie; the Ambassador Bridge in the Detroit area; and the Blue Water Bridge on the Saint Clair River.

To keep the citizens informed, Michigan has 55 daily newspapers, 30 television stations, and 285 radio stations. Newspapers with the largest circulation are the *Detroit News*, the *Detroit Free Press*, the *Grand Rapids Press*, and the *Flint Journal*. Detroit radio station WWJ, which began broadcasting in 1920, is one of the world's oldest commercial radio stations.

Most of Michigan's cattle are raised in the Lower Peninsula.

AGRICULTURE

Along the Lake Michigan shore stretches a fruit belt where delicious cherries, pears, apples, cantaloupes, blueberries, grapes, peaches, and plums grow. Delicate vegetables such as asparagus, celery, sweet corn, and tomatoes grow in the southern Lower Peninsula. Michigan ranks fifth in the country in overall vegetable production. It ranks third in harvesting carrots, celery, and mushrooms. Soil in Michigan's "thumb" has the special quality necessary to grow dry beans of various kinds. Nearly all the nation's navy beans are harvested there. The Upper Peninsula is hampered by a short growing season, but hundreds of dairy farms operate there. Michigan is the nation's sixth-largest producer of milk.

Strangely, Michigan's farms were the source of the state's most dangerous encounter with industrial pollution. In 1973, a

Pumpkins and squash (left) are among the vegetables raised in Michigan, which ranks fifth in the country in overall vegetable production.
Traverse City, famous for its cherries, is also a major producer of apples (above).

poisonous chemical called polybrominated biphenyl (PBB) was mixed by accident into a large supply of livestock feed. Thousands of cattle had to be destroyed. Before the accident was discovered, the poison had spread through the animals' bodies into meat, milk, eggs, and cheese. As many as eight million Michiganders ate the tainted food and became contaminated, to some degree, with the toxic PBB.

In the mid-1990s, Michigan had 52,000 farms, averaging 206 acres (83 hectares) in size. High operating costs and dwindling crop prices have forced many small farmers to hold industrial jobs. Farming is becoming a part-time occupation in Michigan. Farmers who have large debts are in particular trouble. Many farms that have been in the same families for a century or more have been auctioned off to the highest bidder because the owners cannot make their bank payments.

Chapter 9
ARTS AND LEISURE

ARTS AND LEISURE

In Michigan there is plenty for active people to do in their leisure hours. The state has a marvelous assortment of museums, symphony orchestras, and dance bands; a superb school of music and the arts; sports teams; and the huge playground called Michigan Outdoors.

MUSEUMS

The Henry Ford Museum and Greenfield Village complex in Dearborn was founded by Henry Ford I, who said: "When we are through we shall have reproduced American life as lived; and . . . a better and truer impression can be gained than could be had in a month of reading."

Displays in the museum building demonstrate the manner in which technology has changed American life. A hand-cranked washing machine stands next to an electric model built a century later. The museum boasts the finest collection of antique bicycles in America and features nearly two hundred classic cars. Outside spreads Greenfield Village, which is hailed as "240 acres where American history comes to life." The simple farmhouse where Henry Ford was born stands there. Visitors can tour Thomas Edison's laboratory, which was moved—board by board—from its original site in New Jersey.

Among the major works displayed at the Detroit Institute of Arts
is this Diego Rivera mural with an industrial theme.

The Detroit Institute of Arts, established in 1885, has paintings
and sculptures from all over the world. Its prized works are
murals painted by Mexico's master painter Diego Rivera. The
many people of Mexican descent who live in Michigan and visit
the museum leave filled with pride and a sense of their heritage.
Black people feel a similar attachment to the city's Museum of
Afro-American History. The Detroit Historical Museum shows
how the city looked in the 1800s. A bird room and a planetarium
are featured in the Detroit Children's Museum. The Dossin Great
Lakes Museum on Belle Isle displays models of historic ships that
once sailed the lakes.

Scattered throughout the state are museums with various themes. The Grand Rapids Public Museum houses natural-history exhibits. At the Kingman Museum of Natural History in Battle Creek, visitors can study replicas of wildlife and prehistoric animals. The Michigan Historical Museum in Lansing features a "Walk through Time"—a walkway that takes visitors from modern Michigan to the prehistoric era. In the Tower of History at Sault Sainte Marie are models of Great Lakes ships and aquariums stocked with Great Lakes fish. Hartwick Pines State Park has a lumbering museum that exhibits loggers' tools and gives a feel for the life-style of lumberjacks who worked in Michigan's forests a century ago.

THE LITERARY SCENE

One of the first books set in Michigan was *Oak Openings*, by James Fenimore Cooper. The story takes place in the Michigan wilderness during the War of 1812. Describing the forests that towered into the clouds, Cooper wrote, "But God created the woods, and the themes bestowed by his bounty are inexhaustible."

Two writers led Michigan's literary scene during the pioneer era. One was Caroline Kirkland, who emigrated from New York and settled in Pinckney. She found her neighbors to be coarse and shallow people, and made this apparent in her 1839 collection of stories called *A New Home*. Constance Fenimore Woolsen spent her summers on Mackinac Island. Her stories tell of the rugged life endured by settlers of the Upper Peninsula.

Michigan, as well as Minnesota and a few other lumber-producing states, claim Paul Bunyan as a native son. Paul Bunyan was a fantastic lumberjack who, legends say, scooped out the

Great Lakes in order to give his giant blue ox, Babe, a place to drink. Another folk hero, Indian chief Hiawatha, has roots in Michigan. Hiawatha and his wife Minnehaha were created by poet Henry Wadsworth Longfellow in his *Song of Hiawatha*. Longfellow found his inspiration in reports about Indian life written by Michigan pioneer Henry Rowe Schoolcraft.

The state's maritime tradition gave rise to a rich assortment of ballads and sea chanteys, which were usually sung in taverns. Michigan folklorist Ivan H. Walton collected some of the most popular ones and published them in 1940. This selection from Walton's book illustrates the mood of a typical crew:

> In the crew were sons of other lands,
> Roundheads and Scots of a feather,
> Who wandered the world for a drink and a bed
> In fair and stormy weather.

But the life of a Great Lakes sailor was always difficult and dangerous, especially when the "gales of November" howled over the decks of his vessel. The following lines are from a song that laments the steamer *W. H. Gilcher*, which was lost with all its crew in the winter of 1892:

> Lost in Lake Michigan
> They did not reach the shore,
> The gallant ship and crew
> Will sail the lakes no more!

Bruce Catton, a famous historian of the Civil War, was born in 1899 and grew up in Benzonia, Michigan. In an article called "Waiting for the Morning Train," Catton described the beloved land of his boyhood: "Here it is possible to escape from the steamy, overcrowded, overactive middle west and get back to

Michigan-born Bruce Catton and Illinois-born Ernest Hemingway are among the many writers who have been affected by the peace and beauty of Michigan.

something we knew long ago, when it was good enough just to breathe the clean air and feel sunlight and wind on your shoulders."

Many writers born outside the state fell under Michigan's spell during visits. Illinois-born Ernest Hemingway spent his summers in the lake region of northern Michigan and used the setting for several of his early short stories. Modern American writer Joyce Carol Oates, who taught at the University of Detroit in the 1960s, based several novels and short stories in that city.

Malcolm X, the almost mystical leader of the Black Muslims, wrote an interesting and sometimes humorous life story called *The Autobiography of Malcolm X*. Born Malcolm Little, he grew up in Lansing and Mason. His father was a black militant in an era when it was dangerous to take such a stance. When Malcolm was six, his father was beaten to death on the streets of Lansing. The assailants were never brought to justice. In his book, Malcolm X said, "It has always been my belief that I, too, will die by violence." In 1965, Malcolm X was killed by an assassin in New York City.

ARCHITECTURE

The graceful houses built by successful pioneers in the settlements of southern Michigan combined a sense of New England stability with the raw frontier look of the new state. Greek Revival architecture was popular in New England, and its influence can be seen in the 1843 house built in Ann Arbor by Judge Robert S. Wilson. The Honolulu House, an outstanding 1860 house in Marshall, Michigan, has a New England plan with Hawaiian decorations.

Michiganders who earned fortunes in the automobile business built splendid mansions in the Detroit area. One is the 1927 Fisher Mansion along the Detroit River. The residence may be toured, and visitors lucky enough to own a boat may sail through Fisher's private canal and dock at his private pier. Another is the internationally renowned Meadow Brook Hall built by Alfred and Matilda (Dodge) Wilson in 1926-29. The 110-room mansion boasts 35 chimneys and rooms patterned after those in the great houses in England. It is open to visitors. In the Detroit suburb of Grosse Pointe stand some of the nation's most elegant mansions.

Michigan architecture ranges from the ultra-modern Renaissance Center in Detroit (left) to the ornate Honolulu House in Marshall (above).

Many were erected in the 1920s, when wealth generated by the assembly lines produced industrial kings, society queens, and fairy-tale castles.

Detroit's most renowned modern structure is the glittering complex called Renaissance Center. "Ren Cen" is made up of four thirty-nine-story and two twenty-one-story office towers clustered around a seventy-three-story hotel. Inside are seventy shops, four movie theaters, restaurants, lounges, and parking space for six thousand cars. The $337-million center was pushed by Henry Ford II, who involved major Detroit-area corporations in the project, hoping the building would breathe new life into a deteriorating downtown area.

Finnish architect Eliel Saarinen designed the buildings for the Cranbrook Educational Center in Bloomfield Hills. Saarinen, who was associated with Cranbrook for more than twenty years, worked with his son, architect Eero Saarinen, during much of that time.

No architect has left a greater mark on downtown Detroit than Minoru Yamasaki. Born in Seattle, Yamasaki began working in a Detroit architectural firm after World War II. One of his earliest grand efforts was the McGregor Memorial Conference Center at Wayne State University. A truly bold architect, Yamasaki is sometimes playful in his designs. In Detroit, his 1960 Reynolds Metal Company building is surrounded by steel mesh, and his 1962 Michigan Consolidated Gas Company skyscraper has ripples of long, narrow windows. Yamasaki later became one of the principal designers of New York City's World Trade Center, the second-tallest building in the nation.

Stevie Wonder (above) and the Supremes (right) were among the talented musicians discovered by Berry Gordy, Jr., founder of Motown Records.

MUSICAL MICHIGAN

In the 1950s, a young Detroiter named Berry Gordy, Jr. worked on the assembly line at the Ford Motor Company. During his off hours he wrote songs and recorded amateur singing groups. Soon Gordy formed a company called Motown Records. The name comes from a shortening of one of Detroit's nicknames, Motor Town. Gordy's company captured a distinct "Motown sound," a soulful blend of popular music and black gospel.

Gordy had an uncanny knack for discovering fresh talent in the Detroit black community. In 1960, he auditioned three high-school girls who had recently won first prize in a singing competition. They became the pop group known as the Supremes. Led by the golden voice of Diana Ross, the trio recorded twelve number-one national hits in the 1960s. At almost the same time, the blind singer and harmonica player Stevie Wonder came to the Motown Studios. Though he was only thirteen when he began recording, his enormous talent leaped out and captured rock music fans. Motown Records later recorded Michael Jackson and the Jackson Five.

Musical Michigan spreads to all parts of the state—to Holland, where folk-dancing festivals have their roots; to the backwoods of the Upper Peninsula, where old-timers still sing peasant songs they learned from Finnish farmers; to the University of Michigan's School of Music at Ann Arbor. And Michigan has a special institution—unique in the United States—that is devoted to young people and the joy of music. In the northern Lower Peninsula near Traverse City lies the Interlochen Center of the Arts. There gifted elementary and secondary students study general courses, but specialize in music, dance, creative writing, theater, sculpture, and painting.

The school evolved from the National Music Camp, which has met at Interlochen since 1928. Young musicians from all over the world come to this summer camp to perform together in orchestras and form lifelong friendships. Classical music prevails, but students also put on jazz sessions and host an occasional Broadway-type musical. Famous pianist Van Cliburn is a graduate of the camp.

SPORTS

Detroit is the home for baseball's Tigers, football's Lions, hockey's Red Wings, and basketball's Pistons. Most Michigan fans follow these teams. Over the years, the clubs have given their supporters many exciting individual athletes, but very few team championships.

Early in this century, a young Georgia man named Ty Cobb joined the Detroit Tigers. Cobb played baseball with a rare combination of skill and fury. On the field and off he was ill-tempered, foul-mouthed, and quick to start fights. But his baseball achievements were legendary. His career base-hit and stolen-base

Detroit is home to
the American League
Detroit Tigers
baseball team (left).

records stood unchallenged for decades. Al Kaline was a great
Tiger outfielder from the 1950s through the mid-1970s.

Despite having an occasional star player, with a few shining
exceptions the Tigers' record has been mostly mediocre. They won
the World Series in 1945, and again in 1968. In 1984, they opened
the season with an astonishing winning streak and slugged their
way to a World Series victory.

The Detroit Lions were dominant in the 1950s, when they were
led by brilliant quarterback Bobby Layne. Since that time, the
football team has accomplished little.

The hockey Red Wings and the basketball Pistons have also
given their fans exciting individual performers, and even a couple
of titles in recent seasons. Gordie Howe played an amazing
twenty-six seasons in the National Hockey League, all with
Detroit. In 1995, the Red Wings reached the Stanley Cup finals for
the first time in nearly thirty years. The shooting and passing
skills of guard Isiah Thomas led the basketball Pistons to NBA
championships in both the 1988-89 and 1989-90 seasons.

College football is a passion in Michigan, and most attention is
focused on the University of Michigan Wolverines. When the
university plays its traditional rival, Ohio State, a strange hush
falls over both states. Their annual contest is a war. Which school
has the better football program? Fans of both schools will argue
this point at length with anyone.

Winter activities in Michigan include a variety of outdoor sports such as skiing, ski jumping, ice skating, and curling—and there is usually plenty of snow for sleigh rides.

Winter sports have always been popular in this northern state. Young adults from Michigan make up a huge contingent of the national Winter Olympics team. Skiing and ski jumping are favorite activities in the Upper Peninsula. Ice skating is popular in the northern villages and extends even to inner-city Detroit. The winter sport of curling, especially popular in Canada, is played on frozen lakes and in ice rinks. The game calls for one player to slide a pot-shaped stone across the ice while team members equipped with brooms assist the stone along its path by sweeping the ice in front of it. Lacrosse, a fast-paced game derived from an Indian sport, is also a Michigan favorite.

OUTDOOR MICHIGAN

Scattered over Michigan's two peninsulas are ninety-four state parks and recreation areas. This amounts to 250,000 acres (101,172 hectares) of public land devoted to outdoor activities. The lands stretch along 115 miles (185 kilometers) of prime Great Lakes frontage and embrace 200 miles (322 kilometers) of scenic inland lakes and rivers. The parks attract sixteen million visitors each year.

Michigan, with its thousands of inland rivers and lakes and four of the five Great Lakes, is a paradise for the sports fishing enthusiast.

Nearly all the parks and recreation areas offer hiking trails and picnic tables. The parks have thirteen thousand campsites—more than any other state. Some parks and recreation areas offer special activities. Proud Lake Recreation Area in Pontiac, near Detroit, gives city kids the thrill of canoeing down the Huron River.

Though Michigan is an urban state, the people in its towns and cities love the country. In the prosperous 1960s and 1970s, a Detroit factory worker could afford a modest cabin somewhere in the wilds of the north. Detroit is perhaps the only sophisticated big city where fishing can dominate the conversation at business lunches. Those who fish in the state's inland rivers and lakes catch perch, bass, crappie, pike, and trout. Great Lakes anglers try for catfish, sturgeon, lake trout, salmon, and perch.

Hunting is a carefully controlled activity in Michigan. All hunters must be licensed and observe game seasons. Largely because of strict regulations, the state's forests abound with game. Game birds such as pheasants, grouse, and ducks nest in prairie and lake areas.

Chapter 10

HIGHLIGHTS OF THE WOLVERINE STATE

HIGHLIGHTS OF THE WOLVERINE STATE

To see and study every point of interest in Michigan would take a lifetime, but a brief tour of the state's highlights should start in its largest city.

DETROIT

The image of Detroit is in flux. In the early 1980s, unemployment in the city stood at 25 percent. It was estimated that one-third of the city's population received some sort of public aid. With poverty comes crime, street drugs, and racial tension. But a gloomy picture of Michigan's largest city is not entirely accurate. Efforts are being made by the city government and the business community to fight crime and bring jobs back to the urban core.

Coleman Young, Detroit's first black mayor, was elected in 1973. As he took office, he gave this stern message to both street criminals and corrupt police officers: "I issue an open warning now to all those pushers, all rip-off artists, to all muggers. I don't [care] if they are black or white, or if they wear Superfly suits or blue uniforms with silver badges—hit [the] road." Young remained a popular mayor. In 1985 he won a fourth term by defeating Thomas Barrow, a nephew of the still-revered prizefighter Joe Louis. Young held the office until 1993.

Slowly the business community has again begun to invest in Detroit. The sparkling Renaissance Center touched off a $600-

Mount Clemens
Birmingham
Detroit
Dearborn
Wyandotte
Trenton
Grosse Pointe

Detroit scenes

million building boom in the downtown section. The Chrysler Corporation renovated and reopened its Jefferson Avenue plant. A new General Motors plant provided ten thousand jobs. An expanded Cobo Hall will make it the largest convention center in the country, and the new Joe Louis Arena hosts sporting and musical events, as well as conventions and conferences. The downtown is looped by the ultramodern People Mover and an antique trolley line. New lighting will highlight its modern and historic architecture.

Still, impoverished neighborhoods remain a problem. City leaders are criticized frequently for spending money on downtown projects while neighborhoods deteriorate. In some areas, housing is crumbling, and whole square blocks have been reduced to ruins. But citizens' groups have cleaned up many rubbish-strewn lots and joined in crime-watch organizations. While Detroit struggles with its image, thousands of people are proud to call it their home.

DETROIT METROPOLITAN AREA

As the automotive industry expanded in the twentieth century, the population of Detroit and the surrounding area also grew rapidly. The city itself grew right around two smaller cities, Highland Park and Hamtramck, which are now completely surrounded by Detroit.

One of the towns northeast of Detroit is Mount Clemens, once the home of mineral baths that attracted people from all over the nation. Today the town hosts an annual rose festival in August. To the west is Dearborn, where the Ford River Rouge Plant is located. The industrial feeling of River Rouge, Wyandotte, Trenton, and other towns that line the Detroit River is softened by

Detroit's suburban areas include Rochester, where Meadowbrook Hall (left) is located; Grosse Pointe, on Lake Saint Clair (top); and Wayne County (above), southwest of the city.

beautiful riverfront parks. North of Detroit are lovely residential communities such as Bloomfield Hills, Birmingham, and Beverly Hills. Towns east of Detroit, along Lake Saint Clair, include Grosse Pointe, Harper Woods, and Saint Clair Shores.

THE SOUTHERN LOWER PENINSULA

Southern Michigan is known for having towns that could be called the state's "second cities." These southern towns have their own history, character, and economy.

The city of Flint began in 1819 when fur trader Jacob Smith persuaded Indians to surrender the area. In the early 1900s, a large Buick plant opened there. Blacks from the South and Poles from the old country flocked to Flint for jobs. And although Flint suffered the hard times that afflicted the auto industry, the city received help from the C. S. Mott Foundation. Several hundred million dollars were channeled into Flint projects and eased the plight of unemployed auto workers.

Saginaw, north of Flint, grew out of a wilderness fort. During the late 1800s it was a lumber boomtown famous for its hard-drinking, boisterous lumberjacks. Today the city produces cars and auto parts, but it has a more diverse economy than Flint's. Local farmers grow sugar beets that are processed in Saginaw plants. Few other Michigan cities can boast such a close collaboration between farmers and city people.

Michigan's original constitution, written in 1835, declared that the state capital "shall be at Detroit . . . until 1847 when it shall be permanently located by the Legislature." When it was time to choose a new capital, the legislators argued endlessly. Finally, Lansing, which at the time consisted of a sawmill and a few cabins, was suggested and was chosen as a compromise site. The imposing white-domed capitol building, completed in 1879, rises above the city's downtown area. In typical Michigan fashion, factories were built there, too, and the town produced engines, farm tools, and trucks. East Lansing grew around Michigan State University, which began as America's first agricultural college.

Grand Rapids (left), the furniture capital of Michigan and the state's second-largest city, has opera, a symphony, and beautiful parks.

Grand Rapids is Michigan's second-largest city and one of its proudest. It has a diversified economy led by the furniture industry. Fine pieces of sculpture adorn its downtown section. President Gerald Ford grew up there, and a museum honors his achievements. A Grand Rapids restaurant owner recently commented, "I came here from New Jersey, and my friends told me, 'You're moving to the boondocks.' But it's great! We've got opera, good symphony, wonderful parks, safe streets."

Along Interstate 94, west of Detroit, is Ann Arbor, the home of the University of Michigan. Farther west and off the superhighways lie picturesque small towns settled a century ago and hardly touched by industry. Their beauty is known mainly to Michigan residents. Many of these towns center on an old courthouse and an even older church. Their streets are lined with oaks and maples that shade graceful turn-of-the-century houses.

Schoolchildren of the 1930s, 1940s, and 1950s grew up mailing box tops and dimes to Battle Creek, Michigan. The Kellogg and Post Cereal companies sponsored radio programs that gave away such treasured items as a Green Hornet ring that glowed in the dark or a deed to one square inch of Yukon land. To receive one of these prizes, a child had only to send in a box top from the company's product and ten cents for postage. Battle Creek is still the breakfast-cereal capital of the world. Another highlight of the town is the Kellogg Bird Sanctuary, a 100-acre (40.5-hectare) site on Wintergreen Lake that serves as a home for geese, ducks, swans, and other wild birds.

Poets and songwriters have long played with the name "Kalamazoo." A popular song of the 1950s contains the line "From Timbuktu to Kalamazoo." The name that so delights jingle writers comes from an Indian expression meaning "boiling pot." Actually, Kalamazoo is an intellectual and artistic center. It is the home of Western Michigan University, Kalamazoo College, and Nazareth College. The city has a symphony orchestra, art galleries, and several museums.

THE NORTHERN LOWER PENINSULA

The north country is distinguished by its open spaces and natural beauty rather than its towns. It is the Michigan of the farmer, the outdoors sporting enthusiast, and the nature lover.

Near the Au Sable River spreads the Huron National Forest. It is one of the most wildly beautiful lake and forestland areas found anywhere in the Lower Peninsula. Just south of the town of Alpena, the Great Black Rock juts into Lake Huron. It is said that the Ottawa used to place offerings of tobacco on top of this rock in hopes that the gods would protect them on their long canoe trips across the lake.

Sleeping Bear Dunes National Lakeshore

To the west is the Lake Michigan shore, famous for its sand dunes. Few summer visitors can resist kicking off their shoes and scrambling up Sleeping Bear Dune. The sand there is so fine-grained that people sometimes ski down the slopes even in the middle of July. From the top, a climber can look upon North and South Manitou islands. According to Indian folklore, the two islands were once bear cubs who swam too far from shore and drowned. The sand dune itself is the weeping mother bear.

Thick forests grow in the north-central portion of the Lower Peninsula. Hartwick Pines State Park contains a grove of trees that was there long before the European settlers arrived. Somehow, these trees escaped the logger's axe.

The northern tip of the Lower Peninsula is steeped in history. Near the Straits of Mackinac, the French built forts to control the lucrative fur trade. Vacationers at Mackinaw City tour a reconstructed French fort with the tongue-twisting Indian name Michilimackinac. Mackinac Island is now a resort that is unusual in this state so identified with the automobile. No cars are allowed on this four-square-mile (ten-square-kilometer) island. Visitors arrive on ferryboats, and all travel on the island is on foot, by bicycle, in a horse-drawn carriage, or on horseback.

Other islands in northern Lake Michigan include High, Hog, Garden, and Beaver. Beaver Island, the largest, has an interesting history. In 1847 it was settled by a group of Mormons headed by a zealot named James Strang. On this remote island, Strang hoped to develop a religious society isolated from all outside evils. Harsh discipline prevailed in the settlement. Anyone defying Strang's orders was strung up on the community whipping post and flogged. Nine years after the settlement's founding, Strang was shot and killed by rebellious followers.

The last stunning site one encounters in the northern Lower Peninsula is the mighty Mackinac Bridge. For more than a century, engineers dreamed of building a bridge spanning the straits. But wild water and gusting winds discouraged all efforts. Nevertheless, construction began in 1954. After three and a half years of work, and at a cost of almost $100 million, Michigan's two peninsulas were linked by one of the world's longest suspension bridges.

THE UPPER PENINSULA

Father Jacques Marquette established a mission at the town of Saint Ignace in 1671. Just outside Saint Ignace is a museum that

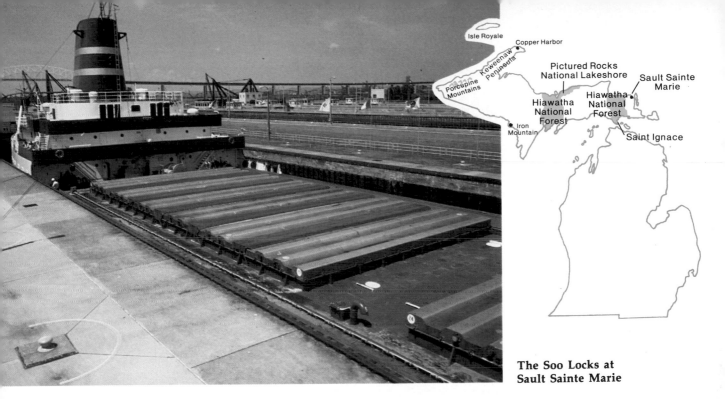

The Soo Locks at Sault Sainte Marie

specializes in information about the life and travels of this Jesuit
priest who dedicated his life to bringing his religion to the
Indians.

The immense Hiawatha National Forest sprawls over the hills
north of Saint Ignace. The name reminds the visitor that the
Upper Peninsula is often called "Hiawatha Country" because the
poet Longfellow set his *Song of Hiawatha* in these thick woodlands.

The city of Sault Sainte Marie is an interesting place to visit.
Tourists can watch massive carrier ships slip silently through the
Soo Locks while entering or leaving Lake Superior. Visitors to the
unusual museum called the Tower of History learn that Sault
Sainte Marie is the oldest continuously occupied European
settlement in all of Michigan.

One of the most spectacular sights in the Upper Peninsula is
Pictured Rocks National Lakeshore. Spreading forty miles (sixty-
four kilometers) along Lake Superior, Pictured Rocks consists of
giant rock formations sculpted by centuries of wind and water

into monuments of fantastic shapes and colors. The vivid colors covering the cliffs lead local people to claim that Pictured Rocks is the "place where Mother Nature cleaned her paintbrushes."

Jutting out into Lake Superior is the Keweenaw Peninsula. Towns with such names as Copper City and Copper Harbor attest that this was once a major copper-mining region. Today, vacationers only whisper about the charms of this corner of the Upper Peninsula. They fear that a flood of tourists and commercialism would come if its glories were discovered. Baraga State Park and the shore of Keweenaw Bay is perhaps the least-known wilderness wonderland in the state.

For the nature lover who wishes to escape civilization, Isle Royale National Park lies only a five-hour boat ride away. No automobiles are allowed, there are no roads (although extensive hiking trails wind through the woods), and hunting is strictly forbidden. The island is one of the last outposts of the North American timber wolf, and also hosts a herd of moose.

South, toward the Wisconsin border, the land is dotted with hundreds of dairy farms, most of which were carved out of the forest by immigrants from Finland. Finnish is still spoken there by many older farmers. A hint of old England is also present because Scottish and Welsh miners once worked in the region's iron mines. In towns such as Iron Mountain, one can buy the hearty bakery item called a Cornish pasty.

Driving west along Route 2, a tourist passes endless lakes with names such as Tamarack, Taylor, Marion, Imp, Crooked, and Clark. Some lakes are too small to be named on a map, but friendly local residents are glad to tell outsiders what they are called. A tourist who asks in a particularly gracious manner might even be told of a secret fishing spot "where you can haul in the really big ones."

Lake of the Clouds in the Porcupine Mountains

At the northwest tip of the Upper Peninsula rise the Porcupine Mountains. These form the only dramatic mountain chain in the state. Nestled among these mountains is the majestic Lake of the Clouds. Trails wind their way to many of the Porcupines' peaks. The walk is exhausting, but the view is magnificent.

Atop the Porcupine Mountains is a fitting place to end a tour of Michigan. From the dizzying cliffs one can look out upon inland rivers and lakes, forests, a scattering of farms, and the endless waters of Lake Superior. Add an industrial city, and the view from the Porcupines would amount to Michigan in a capsule. The state has cities that deafen you, towns that sing to you, lakeshores that awe you, and people who are friendly to you. "Welcome To Michigan" read the signs at its borders. It is a state that leaves visitors enriched.

FACTS AT A GLANCE

GENERAL INFORMATION

Statehood: January 26, 1837, twenty-sixth state

Origin of Name: Michigan is named for Lake Michigan, which the Chippewa called Michigama, meaning "great lake" or "large lake"

State Capital: Lansing; Michigan's first capital was at Detroit, but the state legislature shifted it to Lansing in 1847

State Nickname: "Wolverine State," although no wild wolverines live in Michigan, and, as far as can be determined, the animal has never lived there; early French fur traders probably brought wolverine pelts to Michigan to trade with the Indians; also called the "Water Wonderland" because of its many rivers, lakes, and streams

State Flag: Michigan's banner has a blue field and features a shield flanked by an elk and a moose, both standing proudly on their hind legs. Across the field is the Latin word *Tuebor*, which means "I will defend." Above the shield rises the American eagle, symbolizing the federal government's ultimate authority over the state.

State Motto: *Si quaeris peninsulam amoenam, circumspice*; the Latin words mean, "If you seek a pleasant peninsula, look about you"

State Bird: Robin

State Flower: Apple blossom

State Tree: White pine

State Fish: Brook trout

State Mineral: Petoskey

Tahquamenon
Falls, in
the Upper
Peninsula

State Song: The unofficial state song is "Michigan, My Michigan." The words of one version of the song were written in 1863 by Winifred Lee Brent. The 1902 version by Douglas M. Malloch is more commonly used:

A song to thee, fair State of mine,
Michigan, my Michigan;
But greater song than this is thine,
Michigan, my Michigan;
The whisper of the forest tree,
The thunder of the inland sea;
Unite in one grand symphony
Of Michigan, my Michigan.

I sing a State of all the best,
Michigan, my Michigan;
I sing a State with riches bless'd,
Michigan, my Michigan;
Thy mines unmask a hidden store,
But richer thy historic lore,
More great the love thy builders bore,
Oh Michigan, my Michigan.

How fair the bosom of thy lakes,
Michigan, my Michigan;
What melody each river makes,
Michigan, my Michigan;
As to thy lakes thy rivers tend,
Thy exiled children to thee send
Devotion that shall never end,
Oh Michigan, my Michigan.

Thou rich in wealth that makes a State,
Michigan, my Michigan;
Thou great in things that make us great,
Michigan, my Michigan;
Our loyal voices sound thy claim
Upon the golden roll of fame
Our loyal hands shall write the name
Of Michigan, my Michigan.

POPULATION

Population: 9,295,297, eighth among the states (1990 census)

Population density: 159 people per sq. mi. (61 people per km²)

Population Distribution: 70.5 percent urban, 29.5 percent rural

Detroit	1,027,974
Grand Rapids	189,126
Warren	144,864
Flint	140,761
Lansing	127,321
Sterling Heights	117,810
Ann Arbor	109,592
Livonia	100,850
Dearborn	89,286
Westland	84,724
Kalamazoo	80,277

(Population figures according to 1990 census)

Population Growth: In the last 150 years, Michigan enjoyed tremendous population growth, but in recent years growth has tapered off dramatically. From 1980 to 1990, the state's population increased by only 0.4 percent, compared to a 9.8 percent rise in the national population during the same period. A 1986 U.S. Census Bureau report claimed that Michigan was one of five states that actually lost population the first half of the 1980s. The list below shows the state's population growth since the pioneer era:

Year	Population
1840	212,267
1860	749,113
1880	1,636,937
1900	2,420,982
1920	3,668,412
1930	4,842,325
1940	5,256,106
1950	6,371,766
1960	7,823,194
1970	8,881,826
1980	9,262,078
1990	9,295,297

GEOGRAPHY

The Two Peninsulas: Michigan is divided into the Upper Peninsula and the Lower Peninsula. The Upper Peninsula (U.P.) is about one-fourth the size of the Lower Peninsula. The two peninsulas are separated by the Straits of Mackinac, where Lake Huron and Lake Michigan meet.

Borders: The Upper Peninsula shares a border with Wisconsin. Indiana and Ohio border the Lower Peninsula. Michigan also borders Ontario, Canada.

Highest Point: Mount Arvon in the Upper Peninsula, 1,979 ft. (603 m) (Highest point previously thought to be Mount Curwood)

Lowest Point: Along Lake Erie, 572 ft. (174 m)

Greatest Distances: At its longest points, the Lower Peninsula stretches 286 mi. (460 km) running north and south and 200 mi. (322 km) going east and west. The greatest distances in the Upper Peninsula are 334 mi. (538 km) east to west, and 215 mi. (346 km) north to south.

Area: 58,527 sq. mi. (151,584 km^2)

Rank in Area Among the States: Twenty-third

Rivers: Principal rivers in the Lower Peninsula are the Au Sable, Cass, Clinton, Grand, Huron, Kalamazoo, Manistee, Pere Marquette, Muskegon, Raisin, Saginaw, and Saint Joseph. Upper Peninsula rivers include the Escanaba, Manistique, Menominee, Ontonagan, Sturgeon, Tahquamenon, and Whitefish. Running 260 mi. (418 km), the Grand River is the longest in the state. The Detroit River, which connects Lake Saint Clair with Lake Erie, is a busy shipping lane. Some 150 waterfalls roar and tumble in the Upper Peninsula, but the Lower Peninsula has only one.

Lakes: More than fifteen thousand inland lakes dot Michigan. The largest is Houghton Lake in the north-central portion of the mitten-shaped Lower Peninsula. Other large lakes in the Lower Peninsula are the Black, Burt, Charlevoix, Crystal, Higgins, Mullet, and Torch lakes. Major Upper Peninsula lakes are the Gogebic, the Indian, and the Manistique.

Coasts: Michigan has 3,288 mi. (5,292 km) of shoreline, more than any other inland state. Only Alaska has a greater coastline measurement. Four of the five Great Lakes wash Michigan's shores. Lake Erie touches Michigan in the southeast corner of the state, below Detroit. Above Detroit, Lake Huron sweeps north to the Straits of Mackinac. Lake Michigan has a long and very beautiful shoreline along the western Lower Peninsula and the southern Upper Peninsula. Lake Superior forms the northern shore of the Upper Peninsula.

Islands: Several Great Lakes islands belong to Michigan. The largest is Isle Royale in Lake Superior, which serves as a national park and game reserve. Islands in northern Lake Michigan include Beaver and Manitou. Mackinac Island in the Straits of Mackinac is a popular tourist resort. Nearby are Bois Blanc and Round islands. Drummond Island, in northern Lake Huron, lies off the coast of the Upper Peninsula.

Topography: Michigan's surface is made up primarily of rolling hills rather than lofty mountains. The state's only imposing mountain range is the Porcupine

Natural Arch on
Mackinac Island

Mountain chain on the northwestern tip of the Upper Peninsula. Geologists divide
the state into the Superior Uplands region and the Great Lakes Plains region. The
Superior Uplands run across the western half of the Upper Peninsula and include
the Porcupine Mountains. The Great Lakes Plains, which cover the rest of the state,
are characterized by rolling hills, rivers, and lakes.

Climate: The Upper Peninsula experiences far colder winters than the Lower
Peninsula. The Lower Peninsula is farther south, and is surrounded by Great Lakes
waters that moderate frigid blasts of air. For example, the average January
temperature in Detroit, in the Lower Peninsula, is 32° F. (0° C) for a high and 19° F.
(-7° C) for a low. Escanaba, in the Upper Peninsula, has January temperatures
ranging from a high of 25° F. (-4° C) to a low of 10° F. (-12° C). The lowest
temperature ever recorded in the state was -51° F. (-46° C) at Vanderbilt in 1934,
and highest was 112° F. (44° C) in the town of Mio during the summer of 1936.
Michigan has a moist climate, and large-scale droughts are a rare occurrence.
Spring flooding, on the other hand, is often a problem.

**This beautiful northern Michigan forest is near
Twelvemile Beach at Pictured Rocks National Lakeshore.**

NATURE

Trees: Before the Europeans arrived, nearly all of Michigan except the southern Lower Peninsula was heavily forested. Loggers cut down virtually everything, but second and later tree growth now covers half the state. In the southern Lower Peninsula stand elms, oak, maples, and hickory trees. The vast forests of the north are made up of pines, cedars, firs, and hemlocks, as well as aspens, beeches, birches, maples, and oaks.

Wild Plants: Flowers include the iris, daisy, rose, tiger lily, and orange milkweed. Currants, blackberries, blueberries, raspberries, gooseberries, and elderberries grow wild in many parts of the state. Sunflowers and goldenrod sprout everywhere, even in city lots. Ferns and mosses are found in low-lying areas.

Animals: Deer are found everywhere in Michigan. Black bear are most commonly seen in the forests to the north. A protected herd of elk lives in the northern Lower Peninsula, and a small herd of moose roams Isle Royale. Porcupines, squirrels, rabbits, and chipmunks thrive in Michigan. Fur-bearing animals such as beavers, otters, raccoons, bobcats, skunks, mink, red foxes, and badgers live in the forests.

Birds: Partridge, quail, pheasants, wild geese, and ducks all nest in Michigan.

Fish: In inland rivers and lakes swim bluegills, bass, perch, crappie, pike, muskellunge (muskies), salmon, and trout. In the lake waters off the state's shores are carp, lake herring, smelt, whitefish, sturgeon, lake trout, salmon, and alewives.

GOVERNMENT

As is true with the federal government, the government of Michigan is divided into three branches: executive, legislative, and judicial.

The executive branch is headed by the governor and acts to carry out laws. The state constitution gives the governor the power to send the militia to any area of the state in the event of emergency. The governor also appoints various department heads, but these appointments must be approved by the state senate. The governor may veto an act of the state legislature, but with sufficient votes the legislature can override the veto. The governor is elected for a four-year term and may be reelected any number of times.

The legislative branch is made up of a one-hundred-member house of representatives and a thirty-eight-member senate. The legislature creates new laws or rescinds old ones. Senators serve four-year terms while members of the house are elected to two-year terms.

The judicial branch interprets laws and tries cases. The state supreme court consists of seven justices who are elected to eight-year terms. Lesser courts include an eighteen-judge court of appeals and a circuit court in each of the state's fifty-five judicial districts.

Number of Counties: 83

U.S. Representatives: 16

Electoral Votes: 18

EDUCATION

Michigan spends more on education than on any other item in its budget. It costs the state about $6,500 per year to educate each student. Attendance is compulsory for children between the ages of six and sixteen. In the early 1990s, Michigan had 1,600,000 students enrolled in public elementary and secondary schools.

In its history, Michigan has established many important "firsts" in the field of education. It was first to appoint a superintendent of public instruction, first to provide free primary schools and high schools, and first to establish an agricultural college.

The state supports thirteen public universities and twenty-nine community colleges. Major state-supported universities include the University of Michigan in Ann Arbor, Michigan State University in East Lansing, Wayne State University in Detroit, Michigan Technological University in Houghton, Western Michigan University in Kalamazoo, Eastern Michigan University in Ypsilanti, Central Michigan University in Mount Pleasant, and Northern Michigan University in Marquette.

ECONOMY AND INDUSTRY

Principal Products
Agriculture: Tart cherries, navy beans, cucumbers, blueberries, sweet cherries, apples, plums, carrots, celery, mushrooms, tomatoes for processing, grapes, pears, strawberries, sweet corn, sugar beets, onions, potatoes, dairy products, cattle, hogs, chickens, turkeys
Manufacturing: Motor vehicles and parts, breakfast cereal, furniture, non-electric machinery, chemicals, drugs, machine tools, office machines, athletic equipment, concrete products, photographic equipment
Natural Resources: Iron ore, copper, salt, limestone, petroleum, natural gas, gravel, gypsum, forests, fertile soil, fresh water
Fishing: Michigan's fishing industry is valued at $7.5 million per year. Fish caught commercially in Michigan waters include whitefish, lake trout, chubs, lake herring, perch, catfish, and smelts

Finance: At the turn of the century, Detroit bankers saw a rich market developing in private automobiles, and financed the growth of car companies. Detroit-based banks and insurance companies continue to lead the state in finance.

Tourism: In 1990, tourists brought $16.5 billion into Michigan. Visitors from the crowded cities of Illinois and Ohio enjoy escaping to the wilderness areas of Michigan. Also, residents of southern Michigan towns regularly vacation in the woods and lakes of the northern regions of their state.

Transportation: The nation's first paved concrete highway was built in Detroit in 1909. Today Michigan has about 120,000 mi. (193,000 km) of roads. Railroads were once a vital industry, but today trucks carry three-fourths of the state's goods. Michigan has about three hundred airfields. Detroit's sprawling international airport handles 75 percent of the state's air passengers. During the shipping season, the Detroit River and the locks at Sault Sainte Marie are among the busiest shipping lanes in the world. Detroit is the largest port city, handling 25 million short tons (23 million metric tons) of shipping each year. Michigan's graceful Mackinac Bridge sweeps across the Straits of Mackinac and connects the Upper Peninsula with the Lower Peninsula. Other important bridges are the International Bridge at Sault Sainte Marie, the Ambassador Bridge at Detroit, and the Blue Water Bridge over the Saint Claire River. All of these bridges except the Mackinac link Michigan to Canada.

Communication: Michigan has about 55 daily newspapers, 30 television stations, and 285 radio stations. Leading newspapers include the *Detroit News*, the *Detroit Free Press*, the *Grand Rapids Press*, the *Lansing State Journal,* and the *Flint Journal.*

SOCIAL AND CULTURAL LIFE

Museums: Exhibits in the Henry Ford Museum at Greenfield Village in Dearborn demonstrate the history of technology and how it has changed American life. Structures surrounding the museum building include the simple farmhouse where Henry Ford was born. The city of Detroit hosts the Detroit Institute of Arts, the Museum of Afro-American History, the Detroit Historical Museum, the Children's Museum, and the Dossin Great Lakes Museum on Belle Isle. Other notable museums are the Public Museum and the Gerald Ford Museum in Grand Rapids, the Kingman Museum of Natural History in Battle Creek, the Tower of History in Sault Sainte Marie, and the Michigan Historical Museum in Lansing. Hartwick Pines State Park has a museum devoted to the logging industry.

Libraries: Michigan has 350 public libraries that include 165 branches. With more than 4 million volumes, the University of Michigan at Ann Arbor has the state's largest library. The State Library at Lansing has about 1.25 million books.

Music: Detroit is famous for its very special "Motown Sound," a combination of rock and black gospel music. Detroit also has a fine symphony orchestra. The University of Michigan's School of Music at Ann Arbor is among the finest in the country. At Interlochen is the world-renowned Interlochen Arts Academy and National Music Camp, which bring together talented young musicians.

Sports and Recreation: The state's top professional teams are based in Detroit. They are the Detroit Pistons (basketball), the Detroit Tigers (baseball), the Detroit Lions (football), and the Detroit Red Wings (hockey). These teams have produced some outstanding individual athletes, and even a few championships since the 1980s. In 1984, the Tigers slugged their way to a World Series victory. Michiganders are passionate fans of college football and follow the exploits of their two Big Ten teams, the University of Michigan Wolverines and the Michigan State Spartans. The Wolverines won the coveted Rose Bowl in 1993.

Michigan has ninety-four state parks and recreation areas, which attract about sixteen million visitors each year. The parks have thirteen thousand campsites, more than any other state offers. Fishing is a popular sport throughout the state. Hunting is carefully controlled. Outdoor Michigan is a year-round playground that offers everything from water skiing to tobogganing.

Historic Sites and Landmarks:

Fairlane, on the Henry Ford estate in Dearborn, is an elegant mansion on sprawling grounds that shows the opulent lifestyle of the auto tycoon. The estate is open for public viewing.

Fayette Townsite, near Manistique, was once an Upper Peninsula boomtown that specialized in producing charcoal iron. The village died in the 1890s. Today its crumbling buildings are an industrial ghost town that is fascinating to explore.

Gerald R. Ford Museum is located in Grand Rapids, hometown of the thirty-eighth president. At its opening, President Ford donated many of his most important private papers to the museum.

Because no cars are allowed on Mackinac Island, all travel on the island is on foot, by bicycle, in a horse-drawn carriage, or on horseback.

Fort Wilkins Historical Complex is situated at Copper Harbor in the Upper Peninsula copper region. Buildings and relics of the copper rush remain as symbols of the mining activity that began there in the 1840s. Nearby stands the Copper Harbor Lighthouse, built more than a century ago.

Greenfield Village in Dearborn brings American history to life. Artisans blow glass, forge tools, and make pottery using traditional methods. Artifacts and implements in restored homes and workplaces demonstrate the life-styles of eighteenth-century Americans. Other exhibits emphasize the dramatic change the country underwent as a result of the Industrial Revolution. The many famous buildings that have been brought here from other parts of the country include Thomas Edison's entire Menlo Park Laboratory complex; the Wright brothers cycle shop; the restored nineteenth-century farmhouse and working farm that was the birthplace of tire magnate Harvey Firestone; and the 1860 clapboard farmhouse that was the birthplace of Henry Ford.

Hartwick Pines State Park, near the town of Grayling, contains the only large grove of virgin trees remaining in Michigan. Majestic pines such as these once covered all of northern Michigan. During Michigan's logging era, enough trees were cut down to build ten million six-room houses. The museum at Hartwick Pines shows how loggers lived during the 1800s.

Iron Mountain Iron Mine allows visitors to tour the inside of a working iron mine, where they learn of the importance of mining activity in the Upper Peninsula.

Kalamazoo Water Tower was built in 1895 to serve a mental asylum. The hospital is a story in itself, as there were few facilities to treat the mentally ill in the nineteenth century. The distinctive tower can be seen from any approach to town, and in 1975 the town's residents raised $150,000 to repair the structure rather than tear it down.

Old Fort Mackinac on Mackinac Island and *Fort Michilimackinac* at Mackinaw City have been rebuilt according to their old designs and are open to visitors. Two centuries ago, these forts in the Upper Great Lakes were citadels of power.

Thomas Edison's laboratory at Greenfield Village in Dearborn

Father Marquette Memorial, located near Saint Ignace in the Upper Peninsula, honors the famous priest and explorer. In 1671, Father Marquette founded a mission church on this spot. The nearby museum holds the journals written by the parish priest as he traveled the wilds of North America aboard a canoe.

Michigan Space Center, located in Jackson, is a complex devoted to space exploration. It displays, among other items, the *Apollo 9* capsule that once orbited the earth.

Monroe County Historical Museum, in Monroe, boasts the largest collection of George Armstrong Custer memorabilia in the world. General Custer is famous in history as a bold but somewhat arrogant Indian fighter. Although he is associated with the Wild West, Custer grew up in Michigan.

State Capitol Building, a graceful domed structure rising from the center of downtown Lansing, is a traditional Michigan landmark.

Sojourner Truth's Grave lies near Battle Creek. Many civil-rights activists look upon the grave site of the fiery black abolitionist as a shrine.

Walker Tavern, a venerable inn near Ann Arbor, was built during the stagecoach era. It has been restored to serve as a reminder of Michigan's pioneer past.

White Pine Village is a restored pioneer village near Ludington. The lives of the pioneers who helped build western Michigan are highlighted here.

Other Interesting Places to Visit:

Chapin Mine District in Iron Mountain is an abandoned mining area where a boarding house for bachelor Cornish miners still stands. Chapin Pit is all that remains of the mine after a 1934 cave-in.

Depot Town in Ypsilanti is a historic area that includes the old depot, a renovated freight house, and antique shops.

Edsel and Eleanor Ford House, situated on an 87-acre (35-hectare) estate in Grosse Pointe Shores, is furnished with pieces from all over the world.

Frankenmuth, settled by Germans in the 1840s, still retains a distinctly German atmosphere. A beautiful 35-bell Glockenspiel imported from Germany plays on the hour and depicts the legend of the Pied Piper of Hamelin. Many shops in the downtown area offer Old World craft demonstrations such as woodcarving, glass blowing, and cheese and sausage making. Bonner's Family Christmas Wonderland has the world's largest year-round Christmas display.

Heritage Village in historic Muskegon includes several lumber-era Victorian homes.

Meadow Brook Hall in Rochester, is a beautiful hundred-room Tudor mansion built by Matilda Dodge Wilson. Also on the grounds is Knole Cottage, a six-room playhouse built for the Wilson's daughter.

National Ski Hall of Fame is in Ispheming, the birthplace of organized skiing in America. Two floors of exhibits include national trophies and historic ski equipment.

Sleeping Bear Dunes National Lakeshore at Glen Arbor covers 71,000 acres (28,733 hectares) and includes islands, Lake Michigan shoreline, Sleeping Bear Dunes, a visitors center, and a maritime museum.

Tulip Festival in Holland, a May celebration that takes place when the town's thousands of tulips are in bloom. Visitors can see costumed Holland residents with pails of soapy water scrub the streets as the early settlers of the town did, watch Dutch parades and Dutch dances, and tour the only wooden-shoe factory in the country.

IMPORTANT DATES

10,000 B.C. — The first Michiganders arrive — Indians believed to be descendants of the hunter-gatherers who migrated from Asia to North America over the Bering Strait

3000 B.C. — Early Michiganders learn to make simple tools out of copper

3000 B.C.-A.D. 500 — Mound-building culture spreads into Michigan

Appropriately dressed residents of Holland scrub the streets for the annual tulip festival.

Late 1500s—Indians of the Algonquian-speaking family occupy Michigan

Late 1600s—Three Algonquian-speaking groups—the Potawatomi, the Chippewa, and the Ottawa—rise to prominence; they form a loose confederation called the Three Fires

c. 1618—French explorer Étienne Brulé becomes the first European to visit Michigan

1634—A canoe party led by Jean Nicolet paddles onto the sprawling waters the Chippewa call Michigama, meaning "great lake" or "big lake"

1668—Jesuit priest Jacques Marquette builds a mission at present-day Sault Sainte Marie, the first permanent European settlement in Michigan

1679—The *Griffon* becomes the first vessel other than a canoe to sail the Great Lakes; built by Frenchman René-Robert Cavalier, Sieur de La Salle, the ship is lost on its first voyage in Lake Michigan

1680—The fur trade begins to flourish in the Upper Great Lakes; to control the trade the French build forts at strategic points where all boats must pass

1701—French soldier and fortune-seeker Antoine de la Mothe Cadillac builds a fort at the site of what is now the city of Detroit

1763—French and Indian War ends; British take over the key French forts on the Great Lakes

1763—Ottawa leader Pontiac lays siege to the fort and settlements at Detroit for five months, but is finally forced to withdraw

1783—With Britain defeated in the American Revolution, authority over Michigan passes to the United States, but British forces remain in forts at Detroit and the Straits of Mackinac

1787—Congress combines Michigan and present-day Ohio, Illinois, Indiana, Wisconsin, and parts of Minnesota to form the Northwest Territory

1796—British troops abandon all forts in Michigan

1800—Michigan becomes part of Indiana Territory

1805—Congress creates the Territory of Michigan

1812—The British retake key Michigan forts in the War of 1812

1813—Lewis Cass becomes territorial governor of Michigan, a post he holds for eighteen years; he leads an exploratory mission that covers more than four thousand miles; under Cass's administration, the Indians lose their claim on vast tracts of land

1817—John Jacob Astor founds the American Fur Company, with headquarters on Mackinac Island

1825—The Erie Canal opens in New York State, making travel to and settlement of Michigan far easier

1835—The Territory of Michigan and the state of Ohio fight over ownership of a band of land called the "Toledo Strip"; Congress awards the strip to Ohio, and in consolation gives Michigan the western Upper Peninsula

1837—On January 26, Michigan becomes the twenty-sixth state to be admitted to the Union

c. 1840—Large-scale logging begins; working from south to north, loggers strip the land of trees; the logging era lasts for almost seventy years

1844-45—The copper- and iron-mining boom begins in the Upper Peninsula

During the mid- to late 1800s, Michigan's flourishing logging industry spurred railroad expansion. This lumber train rumbled through the pine forests of the state in 1886, at the height of the boom.

1847—The state capital is moved from Detroit to Lansing

1850—Michiganders vote against an amendment to the state constitution that would give blacks the right to vote

1854—The Republican party, which was based on a strong anti-slavery platform, holds early meetings in the town of Jackson

1855—The Soo Ship Canal and Locks are completed

1860—The Civil War breaks out and Michiganders rally behind President Lincoln and the Union cause; some ninety thousand Michigan men serve in the war, fourteen thousand lose their lives

1865—Railroad construction flourishes; railroads had already operated for more than three decades in Michigan, but the industry's boom time came in the late 1800s

1883—Boats ferry railroad cars across the Straits of Mackinac to form a railroad link between the two peninsulas

In 1908, Henry Ford marketed the first Model T automobile.

1894 — In Battle Creek, C. W. Post markets a breakfast drink called Postum; four years later he produces Grape-Nuts and is on the road to becoming a millionaire

1896 — Henry Ford builds his first automobile, in Detroit

1899 — Ransom E. Olds opens Michigan's first automobile factory, in Detroit

1903 — Henry Ford organizes the Ford Motor Company

1905 — W. K. Kellogg starts a food-processing company in Battle Creek that specializes in making breakfast cereals

1908 — Henry Ford markets the first Model T, which quickly becomes the world's most popular automobile; William C. ("Billy") Durant combines several car companies to form the industrial giant General Motors

1909 — Michigan builds America's first concrete highway, a mile-long roadway in Detroit

1914 — Henry Ford shocks the industrial world by raising the wages of his workers to five dollars per day

1917 — Michigan industrial plants produce ships, shells, trucks, and engines for the World War I fighting fronts

The Mackinac Bridge,
linking the Upper
and Lower Peninsulas,
was opened in 1957.

1930—Census reports reveal that 68 percent of Michiganders live in cities and towns; Detroit's population has grown to more than 1.5 million

1932—Because of the Great Depression, one out of three workers in Detroit has no job

1935—Michigan workers and union leaders organize the United Auto Workers (UAW)

1936—Labor strikes rock Michigan factories

1937—General Motors, Chrysler, and other auto manufacturers agree to recognize the UAW as their employees' sole bargaining agent

1942—Michigan's factories produce vast quantities of war material

1943—The bloodiest race riot of the World War II years breaks out in Detroit

1948—Walter Reuther, head of the UAW, secures a labor agreement with Chrysler

1957—The Mackinac Bridge linking the Upper and Lower Peninsulas is opened

1963—Voters ratify Michigan's fourth state constitution

Coleman Young, the first black mayor of the city of Detroit, was first elected in 1973.

1967—Forty-three people die and hundreds are arrested during several nights of racial unrest in Detroit

1973—Sales of large Detroit-made cars suffer because of gasoline shortage

1973—Coleman Young, Detroit's first black mayor, is elected; the toxic chemical PBB is accidentally mixed with animal feed and given to thousands of Michigan farm animals; the animals are destroyed, but the chemical lingers in the land and eventually contaminates people

1983—Statewide unemployment reaches 17 percent

1985—Coleman Young wins a fourth term as mayor of Detroit

1986—A United States Census Bureau report claims that Michigan is one of only five states to have a net loss of population in the first half of the 1980s

1987—Michigan celebrates its sesquicentennial

1988—City Airport in Detroit opens to major commercial flights; the automobile industry achieves its third-best sales year in history

1990—Automakers record their steepest production drop in nearly a decade; building continues on three Michigan-based Japanese automotive-research and technical facilities

1994—Michigan voters approve a higher state sales tax; Dennis Archer is elected Detroit's new mayor

IMPORTANT PEOPLE

John Jacob Astor (1763-1848), German-born fur-trader and real estate tycoon, possibly the richest man of his era; primarily associated with New York, but his American Fur Company had a powerful impact on Michigan and the Upper Great Lakes

Liberty Hyde Bailey (1858-1954), born in South Haven; botanist; graduated from the Michigan State Agricultural College (now Michigan State University); encouraged agricultural education in the United States; taught for many years at New York's Cornell University, where he founded the Bailey Hortorium

Étienne Brulé (1592-1632), French-born explorer and adventurer, probably the first European to see the land that is now Michigan

Ralph Bunche (1904-1971), born in Detroit; statesman; in 1950 became the first American black to be awarded the Nobel Peace Prize; helped found the United Nations; served in various United Nations undersecretary posts (1955-71)

Antoine de la Mothe Cadillac (1656-1730), French explorer; territorial official in Michigan and Louisiana; founded the city of Detroit in 1701; wrote memoirs that have become valuable tools for historians

Will Carleton (1845-1912), born and raised in Michigan; poet; his first poetry collection, *Farm Ballads*, brought him national attention; moved to Boston and eventually to Brooklyn, New York, where he founded poetry magazine *Every Where*

Lewis Cass (1782-1866), governor of the Territory of Michigan (1813-31); organized and led a canoe trip to explore the territory; Democratic nominee for president of the United States (1848)

Charles Bruce Catton (1899-1978), born in Petoskey; author, historian; known mainly for Civil War books; his book *Michigan* appeared in the bicentennial series "The States and the Nation"

Tyrus Raymond (Ty) Cobb (1886-1961), baseball player, manager; played twenty-two years with Detroit Tigers, the last six years of which he also managed the team; probably was the greatest baseball player of his time, but often had a nasty temper; said one of his teammates, "He had such a rotten disposition it was darned hard to be his friend"

Charles Edward Coughlin (1891-1979), Roman Catholic priest; known as the "radio priest" during the 1930s, commanded a wide audience while broadcasting from his Detroit station; broadcast his extreme opinions on labor, economics, and politics; strongly anticommunist, was rebuked by Catholic Church leaders when his views became increasingly anti-Jewish

RALPH BUNCHE

BRUCE CATTON

TY COBB

FATHER COUGHLIN

GEORGE A. CUSTER

THOMAS E. DEWEY

WILLIAM DURANT

GERALD R. FORD

James Joseph Couzens (1872-1936), industrialist, political leader, philanthropist; mayor of Detroit (1919-22); United States Senator (1922-36); helped found the Ford Motor Company, served as an executive of the firm; once donated $10 million to a children's-aid fund

James Oliver Curwood (1878-1927), born in Owosso; author; wrote twenty-six novels, most of them about rugged life in the northwestern United States; had an immense following around the turn of the century; built a palatial house in Owosso, where he lived until his death

George Armstrong Custer (1839-1876), army officer; spent much of his childhood in Michigan; during the Civil War became a general at age twenty-three; famous for his bravery in battle, but many fellow officers believed him to be a "glory hound"; killed by Indian warriors at the Battle of the Little Big Horn in Dakota Territory

Thomas Edmund Dewey (1902-1971), born in Owosso; lawyer, politician; district attorney of New York county (1937-38); governor of New York (1943-55); Republican nominee for president of United States (1944, 1948)

John Francis Dodge (1864-1920), and **Horace Elgin Dodge** (1868-1920), born in Niles; in their youth started a company that built bicycles; later made auto parts for the Ford and Olds companies; in 1914 they produced their own car, and Dodge became a household name

Herbert Henry Dow (1866-1930), chemist and manufacturer; founder of Dow Chemical Company, Midland

William Crapo ("Billy") Durant (1861-1947), industrialist; pioneer in mass production; called the "Godfather of the Automobile Industry"; combined several companies to form General Motors

Gerald Rudolph Ford (1913-   ), thirty-eighth president of the United States; came to Grand Rapids at age of two; graduated from the University of Michigan; named most-valuable player on the school's football team; became an attorney; served in the United States Navy (1942-46); served in the United States House of Representatives (1948-73); named vice-president by President Richard Nixon upon resignation of Spiro Agnew (1973); became president eight months later after Nixon resigned under the burden of the Watergate scandal; lost a close presidential election to Jimmy Carter in 1976

Henry Ford I (1863-1947), born in Dearborn; automobile manufacturer; built an automobile in 1896; founded the Ford Motor Company, introduced the Model T car, and became a millionaire; fought bitter battles with organized labor unions; donated millions of dollars to the philanthropic Ford Foundation

Henry Ford II (1917-1987), born in Detroit; grandson of Henry Ford; became president of the Ford Motor Company in 1945; reorganized the failing company to make it profitable again; active in many Detroit projects, including the building of the Renaissance Center

Berry Gordy, Jr. (1929-   ), born in Detroit; record company and motion-picture executive; founded Motown Record Corporation in 1959 and began recording black singers and musical groups; recorded artists such as Diana Ross and the Supremes, Michael Jackson and the Jackson Five, Stevie Wonder, and Marvin Gaye

Martha Griffiths (1912-   ), politician; the first woman in Michigan to be elected lieutenant governor (1982)

Edgar Albert Guest (1881-1959), journalist, poet; on staff of *Detroit Free Press*; author of popular verse

Tom Harmon (1919-1990), 1930s football star at the University of Michigan; radio and television announcer

TOM HARMON

Gordie Howe (1928-   ), Canadian-born hockey player; played twenty-six seasons with the Detroit Red Wings; set many hockey records and helped make the Red Wings a powerhouse team in the 1950s

Lido Anthony (Lee) Iacocca (1924-   ), automotive manufacturing executive; chairman of the board and chief operating officer, Chrysler Corporation, Highland Park

GORDIE HOWE

Al Kaline (1934-   ), baseball player; outfielder for the Detroit Tigers from 1953 to 1975; sharp hitter, speedy base runner, and consistent American League All Star

John Harvey Kellogg (1852-1943), born in Tyrone; physician; superintendent of Battle Creek Sanitarium, where his brother William developed dry breakfast cereals

William Keith Kellogg (1860-1951), born in Battle Creek; manufacturer, philanthropist; developed and marketed the cornflake; as head of the original Kellogg Company of Battle Creek, became a millionaire; founded the W.K. Kellogg Foundation

LEE IACOCCA

Sebastian Spering (S.S.) Kresge (1867-1966), merchant; founder of S.S. Kresge variety stores (now K mart Corporation); established the nonprofit Kresge Foundation, Troy

Paul Henry de Kruif (1890-1971), born in Zeeland; bacteriologist, author; bacteriologist at Rockefeller Institute (1920-22); two of his best-known books are *Microbe Hunters* and *Man Against Insanity*

Charles Augustus Lindbergh (1902-1974), born in Detroit; aviator; made the first solo nonstop transatlantic flight (1927) in *The Spirit of St. Louis*

AL KALINE

JOE LOUIS

FRANK MURPHY

JOYCE CAROL OATES

WALTER REUTHER

Joe Louis (1914-1981), born Joe Louis Barrow; boxer; came to Detroit as a child; held the heavyweight title from 1937 to 1949; fought twenty-five times as champion, scored twenty knockouts; world famous in the 1940s, was looked upon as a symbol of hope by American blacks

Malcolm X (1925-1965), born Malcolm Little; black nationalist leader; grew up in the Lansing area; a mesmerizing public speaker; became one of the most influential Americans of his time

Stevens T. Mason (1811-1843), Michigan's first governor; inaugurated at age twenty-four; was called the "boy governor"

Carl Milles (1875-1955), Swedish-born sculptor; his statues and monuments decorate plazas in cities throughout the world; taught sculpture at the Cranbrook Academy of Art near Detroit

Charles Stewart Harding (C.S.) Mott (1906-   ), philanthropist, foundation executive; chairman and chief executive officer of the Mott Foundation of Flint

William Francis (Frank) Murphy (1893-1949), born in Harbor Beach; politician, jurist; became mayor of Detroit in 1930; elected governor of Michigan in 1936; appointed United States Attorney General in 1939; became a justice of the Supreme Court in 1940; was a strong defender of civil liberties while serving on the court

Joyce Carol Oates (1938-   ), award-winning novelist; taught in Detroit in the 1960s; used Michigan as a setting for many of her stories and novels

Ransome Eli Olds (1864-1950), machinist and inventor; first to mass produce cars; produced the Oldsmobile in his Detroit factory

Chase Salmon Osborn (1860-1949), governor of Michigan (1911-13); earlier, was a newspaperman and a postmaster in the Upper Peninsula; entered politics as Michigan's game and fish warden and fought to preserve Michigan's woodlands

Hazen S. Pingree (1840-1901), politician; mayor of Detroit (1890-96) governor of Michigan (1897-1900); as mayor, lowered Detroit utility rates and abolished tolls on roads into the city; as governor, fought to require powerful railroad companies to pay a fair share of the tax burden

Charles William Post (1854-1914), food manufacturer and labor union opponent; concocted a coffee substitute made of molasses and bran and marketed it under the name Postum; developed various breakfast foods, which he produced in his factories in Battle Creek

Walter Reuther (1907-1970), labor organizer; president of United Auto Workers from 1946 until his death; negotiated contracts with the auto companies to give medical and pension benefits to workers; also president of a powerful coalition of unions called the Congress of Industrial Organizations (CIO)

George Romney (1907-1995), politician; president of the American Motors Company before entering politics; served as governor from 1963 to 1969; was a leading Republican candidate for president of United States in 1968

Diana Ross (1944-   ), born in Detroit; singer, actress; led the popular singing group called the Supremes; won praise for her portrayal of Billie Holiday in the 1972 movie *Lady Sings the Blues*

DIANA ROSS

Henry Rowe Schoolcraft (1793-1864), geologist; member of the Michigan exploratory mission led by Lewis Cass in 1820; later served as federal agent for Lake Superior-area Indians; wrote both literary and scientific works that are valuable sources of information on Indian history, culture, and traditions

Tom Selleck (1945-   ), born in Detroit; actor; best known for starring role in television series "Magnum P.I."

Isiah Thomas (1961-   ), basketball player; played guard for the Detroit Pistons; known for his smooth moves on the basketball court; voted the Most Valuable Player in the NBA All Star Game in 1986, the second time he won that honor

A. H. VANDENBERG

Lily Tomlin (1939-   ), born in Detroit; actress; television credits include "The Music Scene" and "Laugh In"; motion pictures include *The Incredible Shrinking Woman* and *Nine to Five*; appeared in one-woman broadway shows "Appearing Nitely" and "The Search for Signs of Intelligent Life in the Universe"

Sojourner Truth (1797-1863), born a slave named Isabella; evangelist and reformer; freed by New York's 1827 Emancipation Act; traveled the country preaching against slavery; later settled in Battle Creek

Albertus Van Raalte (1811-1876), Dutch preacher; led a group of his associates from a small town in the Netherlands to the New World; they founded Holland, Michigan, and many waves of Dutch settlers followed

G. MENNEN WILLIAMS

Arthur Hendrick Vandenberg (1884-1951), born in Grand Rapids; politician; Republican United States senator; gave vital support to President Harry Truman's foreign policy in the years after World War II; helped organize the United Nations

G. Mennen Williams (1911-1988), born in Detroit; justice, politician; governor of Michigan (1949-60). Considered a front-line candidate for United States president in 1960, but lost to the highly popular John F. Kennedy; served the Kennedy administration as assistant secretary of state for African Affairs; chief justice of state supreme court

Stevie Wonder (1950-   ), born Steveland Judkins Morris in Saginaw; singer, musician, composer; "Little Stevie" Wonder began making records when he was thirteen; had produced fourteen gold singles, four gold albums, and two platinum albums by the mid-1970s

STEVIE WONDER

MINORU YAMASAKI

Minoru Yamasaki (1912-1986), architect; came to Detroit in 1945; designed many of Detroit's outstanding buildings

Coleman Young (1918-   ), Detroit's first black mayor; elected in 1973 and held the office for twenty years; succeeded in persuading business leaders to invest in Detroit

GOVERNORS

Stevens T. Mason	1837-1840	Fred M. Warner	1905-1911
William Woodbridge	1840-1841	Chase S. Osborn	1911-1913
James W. Gordon (acting)	1841-1842	Woodbridge N. Ferris	1913-1917
John 5. Barry	1842-1846	Albert E. Sleeper	1917-1921
Alpheus Felch	1846-1847	Alexander J. Groesbeck	1921-1927
William L. Greenly	1847-1848	Fred W. Green	1927-1931
Epaphroditus Ransom	1848-1850	Wilbur M. Brucker	1931-1933
John 5. Barry	1850-1852	William A. Comstock	1933-1935
Robert McClelland	1852-1853	Frank D. Fitzgerald	1935-1937
Andrew Parsons	1853-1855	Frank Murphy	1937-1939
Kingsley S. Bingham	1855-1859	Frank D. Fitzgerald	1939
Moses Wisner	1859-1861	Luren D. Dickinson	1939-1941
Austin Blair	1861-1865	Murray D. Van Wagoner	1941-1943
Henry H. Crapo	1865-1869	Harry F. Kelly	1943-1947
Henry P. Baldwin	1869-1873	Kim Sigler	1947-1949
John L. Bagley	1873-1877	G. Mennen Williams	1949-1961
Charles H. Croswell	1877-1881	John B. Swainson	1961-1963
David H. Jerome	1881-1883	George W. Romney	1963-1969
Josiah W. Begole	1883-1885	William G. Milliken	1969-1983
Russell A. Alger	1885-1887	JamesJ. Blanchard	1983-1991
Cyrus G. Luce	1887-1891	John Engler	1991-
Edwin B. Winans	1891-1893		
John T. Rich	1893-1897		
Hazen 5. Pingree	1897-1901		
Aaron T Bliss	1901-1905		

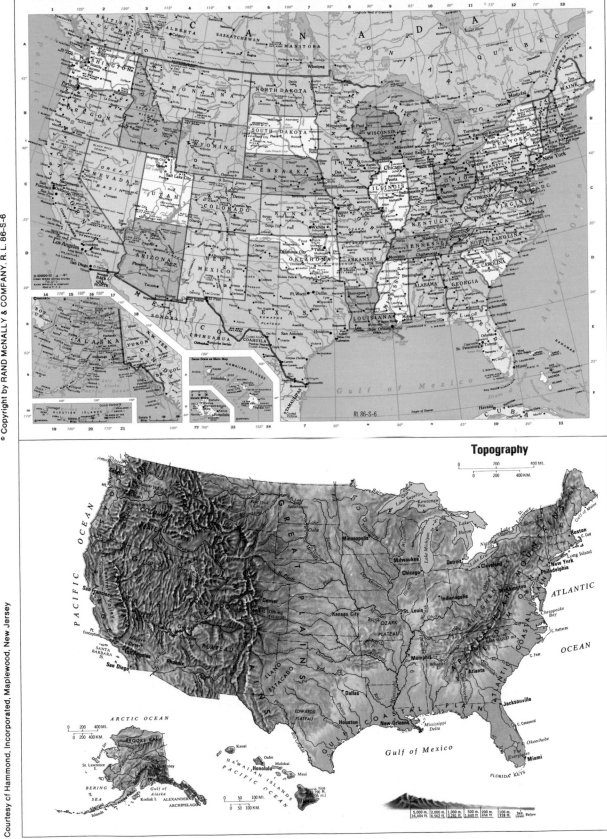

Topography

MAP KEY

Adams Point (point)	C7	East Lansing	F6	Kalamazoo	F5	Pine River (river)	D5

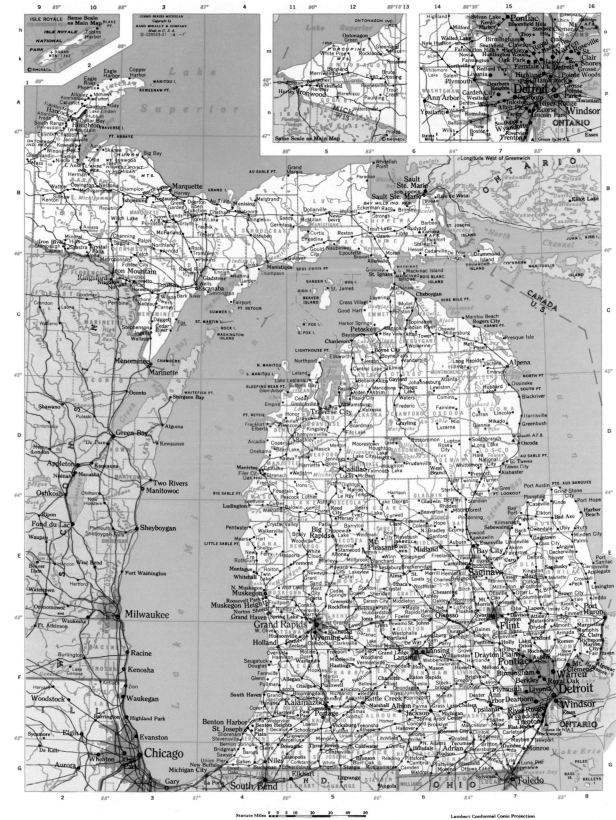

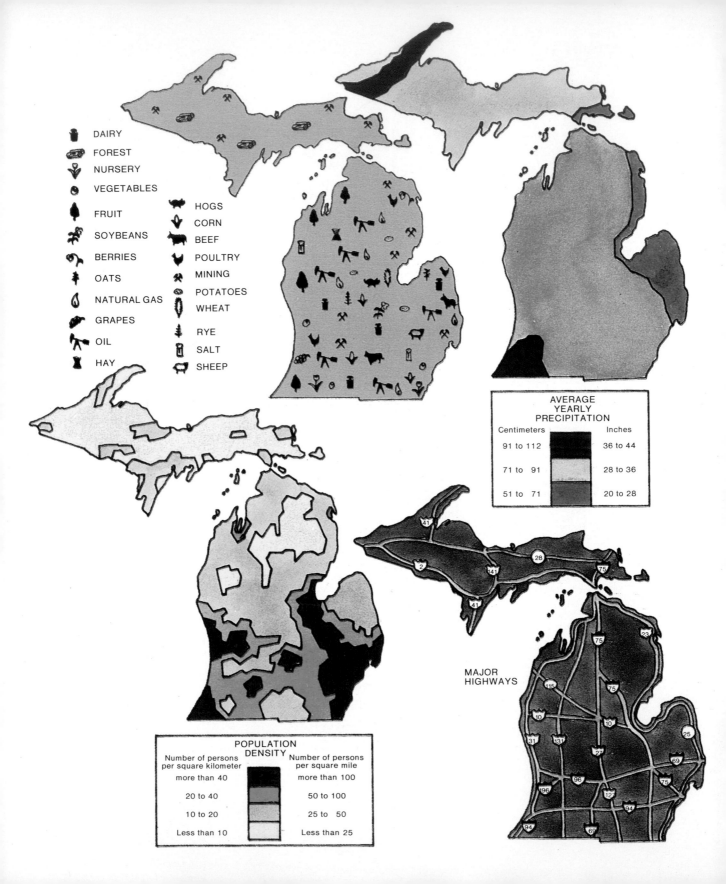

DAIRY
FOREST
NURSERY
VEGETABLES
FRUIT
SOYBEANS
BERRIES
OATS
NATURAL GAS
GRAPES
OIL
HAY

HOGS
CORN
BEEF
POULTRY
MINING
POTATOES
WHEAT
RYE
SALT
SHEEP

AVERAGE YEARLY PRECIPITATION

Centimeters	Inches
91 to 112	36 to 44
71 to 91	28 to 36
51 to 71	20 to 28

MAJOR HIGHWAYS

POPULATION DENSITY

Number of persons per square kilometer	Number of persons per square mile
more than 40	more than 100
20 to 40	50 to 100
10 to 20	25 to 50
Less than 10	Less than 25

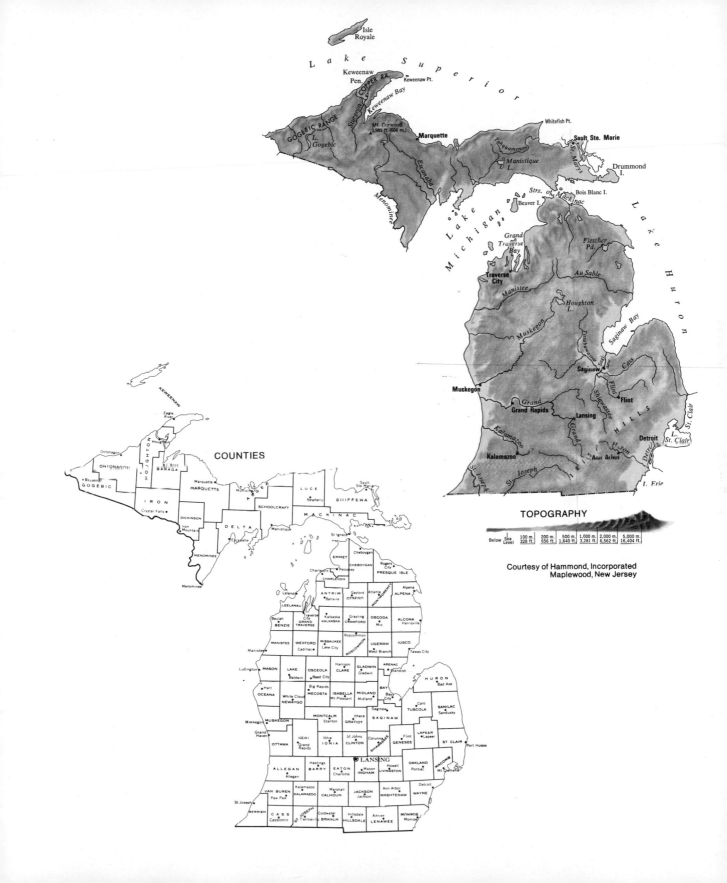

Isle
Royale

L a k e   S u p e r i o r

Keweenaw
Pen.
COPPER RA.
Keweenaw Pt.

Keweenaw Bay

GOGEBIC RANGE

L.
Gogebic

Mt. Curwood
1,980 ft. (604 m.)

Marquette

Whitefish Pt.

Sault Ste. Marie

Drummond
I.

Escanaba

Tahquamenon

*Manistique
L.*

Menominee

Strs. of Mackinac

Bois Blanc I.

Beaver I.

L a k e

M i c h i g a n

L a k e   H u r o n

Grand
Traverse
Bay

Fletcher
Pd.

Traverse
City

Au Sable

Manistee

Houghton
L.

Muskegon

Saginaw Bay

Tittabawassee

Saginaw

Cass

Muskegon

Grand

Grand Rapids

Lansing

Shiawassee

Flint

H I L L S

Detroit

L.
St. Clair

St. Clair

Kalamazoo

Grand

Kalamazoo

Huron

Ann Arbor

Detroit

St. Joseph

St. Joseph

L. Erie

TOPOGRAPHY

Below Sea Level	100 m. 328 ft.	200 m. 656 ft.	500 m. 1,640 ft.	1,000 m. 3,281 ft.	2,000 m. 6,562 ft.	5,000 m. 16,404 ft.

Courtesy of Hammond, Incorporated
Maplewood, New Jersey

COUNTIES

KEWEENAW

Eagle
River

Houghton

Ontonagon

ONTONAGON

HOUGHTON

BARAGA

Bessemer

GOGEBIC

Marquette

MARQUETTE

Munising

ALGER

Sault
Ste Marie

LUCE

SCHOOLCRAFT

CHIPPEWA

IRON

Crystal Falls

DICKINSON

Iron
Mountain

DELTA

Newberry

Escanaba

MACKINAC

Manistique

St Ignace

MENOMINEE

Menominee

EMMET

Cheboygan

Charlevoix

Petoskey

CHEBOYGAN

Rogers
City

PRESQUE ISLE

CHARLEVOIX

Leland

LEELANAU

ANTRIM

Bellaire

Gaylord

OTSEGO

Atlanta

MONTMORENCY

ALPENA

Alpena

Beulah

BENZIE

Traverse
City

GRAND
TRAVERSE

Kalkaska

KALKASKA

Grayling

CRAWFORD

OSCODA

Mio

ALCONA

Harrisville

MANISTEE

Manistee

WEXFORD

Cadillac

MISSAUKEE

Lake City

Roscommon

ROSCOMMON

OGEMAW

West Branch

IOSCO

Tawas City

Ludington

MASON

LAKE

Baldwin

OSCEOLA

Reed City

Harrison

CLARE

GLADWIN

Gladwin

ARENAC

Standish

HURON

Bad Axe

Hart

OCEANA

White Cloud

NEWAYGO

Big Rapids

MECOSTA

ISABELLA

Mt Pleasant

MIDLAND

Midland

BAY

Bay
City

Caro

TUSCOLA

SANILAC

Sandusky

Muskegon

MUSKEGON

MONTCALM

Stanton

Ithaca

GRATIOT

SAGINAW

Saginaw

Grand
Haven

OTTAWA

KENT

Grand
Rapids

IONIA

Ionia

St Johns

CLINTON

Corunna

SHIAWASSEE

Flint

GENESEE

LAPEER

Lapeer

ST CLAIR

Port Huron

LANSING

Hastings

BARRY

EATON

Charlotte

Mason

INGHAM

Howell

LIVINGSTON

Pontiac

OAKLAND

MACOMB

Mt Clemens

Detroit

ALLEGAN

Allegan

Kalamazoo

KALAMAZOO

Marshall

CALHOUN

JACKSON

Jackson

Ann Arbor

WASHTENAW

WAYNE

St Joseph

BERRIEN

VAN BUREN

Paw Paw

CASS

Cassopolis

ST JOSEPH

Centreville

Coldwater

BRANCH

Hillsdale

HILLSDALE

Adrian

LENAWEE

MONROE

Monroe

The Point Betsie Lighthouse near Frankfort

INDEX

Page numbers that appear in boldface type indicate illustrations

139

Tulip time in Holland

141

Picture Identifications

Front cover: Renaissance Center, Detroit
Back cover: Skiing in Michigan
Pages 2-3: Hoffmaster State Park
Page 6: M!ch!gan hot-air balloon
Pages 8-9: A southern Michigan lake
Page 20: Montage of Michigan residents
Page 28: An archaeological dig on Mackinac Island
Pages 34: Father Jacques Marquette with a *calumet*, or peace pipe
Pages 42-43: Breaking a log jam
Page 54: An early Ford automobile
Page 70: The state capitol at Lansing
Page 80: The Henry Ford Museum in Dearborn
Page 94 (inset): The Lake Superior shoreline at Pictured Rocks National Lakeshore
Pages 94-95: A Michigan forest in the autumn
Page 108: Montage showing the state flag, the state tree (white pine), the state bird (robin), the state stone (petoskey), and the state flower (apple blossom)

Picture Acknowledgments

Journalism Services: © John Patsch: Front cover; © Rick Hayes: Page 79 (right)
H. Armstrong Roberts: Pages 24 (left), 45 (right), 52 (top left), 68 (top); © Camerique: Back cover, page 18; © O'Neill: Page 4; © H. Lamberth: Pages 8-9; © David Muench: Pages 94-95; © K. Vreeland: Page 121; © R. Krubner: Page 108 (top right)
© **Reinhard Brucker:** Pages 2-3, 14 (left), 38
Nawrocki Stock Photo: © Sylvia Schlender: Pages 5, 6, 13, 20 (top right), 23 (left), 68 (bottom right), 78, 79 (left), 85, 92, 101; ©Jeff Apoian: Page 16 (right); © Robert M. Lightfoot: Page 119
© **Joan Dunlop:** Pages 11 (left), 52 (top right)
© **Joseph Antos:** Pages 11 (right), 107
Tom Stack & Associates: © Larry Deck: Page 14; © Gary Milburn: Page 108 (top left)
R/C Photo Agency: © Betty A. Kubis: Page 15; © Richard L. Capps: Page 28
© **Reidar Hahn:** Pages 16, 20 (bottom left)
Roloc Color Slides: Page 19
EKM-Nepenthe: © Ron Cooper: Page 20 (top left); © MacDonald: Page 20 (bottom right); © Robert V. Eckert Jr.: Pages 25, 87 (right), 97 (right), 99 (top right); © John R. Maher: Page 97 (bottom)
© **W. Ray Scott:** Pages 20 (middle), 22 (both photos), 31, 93 (left), 97 (top left), 103
Photri: Pages 32 (both photos), 108 (bottom left), 124; © MacDonald: Page 23; © Ken Kaminsky: Page 68 (middle); © R.C.W. Biedel, FPSA: Page 105
© **Brent Jones:** Pages 24 (right), 89 (left), 141
Root Resources: © James Blank: Pages 25 (right), 87 (left); © Lia Munson: Page 94 (inset)
Historical Pictures Service, Inc., Chicago: Pages 34, 37, 41 (left), 42-43, 46, 47, 65
The Bettmann Archive: Pages 41 (right), 45, 50, 52 (middle right and bottom), 57 (bottom), 58 (left), 62, 89 (right), 123
UPI/Bettmann: Pages 61, 66, 127 (Cobb and Coughlin), 131 (Ross)
© **Jerry Hennen:** Page 52 (middle left)
Wide World Photos: Pages 57 (top left), 127 (Bunche and Catton), 128 (all photos), 129 (all photos), 130 (all photos), 131 (Vandenberg, Williams, and Wonder), 132
© **Virginia Grimes:** Pages 57 (top right and middle right), 113, 118
Courtesy Michigan Travel Bureau: Pages 58 (right), 72 (left), 88
© **The Photo Source:** Pages 70, 75, 80, 138
© **Cameramann International Ltd.:** Pages 54, 72 (right), 76, 85 (inset), 91, 93 (right), 125
© **Chandler Forman:** Page 82
© **Doris Scharfenberg:** Pages 99 (left and bottom right), 108 (tree)
Valan Photos: © Wayne Lankinen: Page 110
Bob and Ira Spring: © Kirkendall: Page 114
Detroit Department of Public Information: Page 126
Len W. Meents: Maps on pages 97, 101, 103, 105, 136
Courtesy Flag Research Center, Winchester, Massachusetts 01890: Flag on page 108

About the Author

R. Conrad Stein was born and grew up in Chicago. While studying at the University of Illinois, he worked on iron ore-carrying ships that plied the waters of the Great Lakes. Often these "ore boats" sailed along the coast of the state of Michigan, and stopped at Michigan's many industrial ports. After graduating from college, Mr. Stein became a professional writer, and Michigan was his favorite vacationland. He is particularly fond of the wilds of the Upper Peninsula. Mr. Stein is the author of many books, articles, and short stories written for young people.